dictionary
of reading
and learning
dis·a·bil·i·ty

by
Clifford L. Bush, Ed.D.
and
Robert C. Andrews, M.A.

Published by

WESTERN PSYCHOLOGICAL SERVICES
PUBLISHERS AND DISTRIBUTORS
12031 WILSHIRE BOULEVARD
LOS ANGELES, CALIFORNIA 90025
A DIVISION OF MANSON WESTERN CORPORATION

International Standard Book Number: 0-87424-153-7

Library of Congress Catalog Card Number: 79-57293

Second Printing .... October 1980

PREFACE
Scope
This dictionary was compiled by the authors to serve teachers in the fields of reading and learning disabilities. Much of their diagnostic and remedial work must deal with related disciplines. Terms were added from the following: measurement, evaluation, and statistics; linguistics; library science; psychology and learning; education; and medicine, particularly dealing with visual, sensory, and motor functions. Definitions given are those relevant to reading and learning disabilities.

Rationale
Teachers in the reading and learning disabilities field are busy people and they need assistance in dealing with terms from all the above disciplines. Their inter-disciplinary communication of facts and ideas can be enhanced by a quick, ready reference. Most of them have limited personal libraries, and they find that access to a large library with specialized reference sources is inconvenient and time-consuming. This dictionary was designed in size, content, and scope to meet their day-to-day needs as a handy reference, as they read the professional books and journals, interpret an educational program from referral specialists, or become involved in educational study.

Guidelines for Use
The entries are alphabetized. If there are two words in the entry or if it is a compound, the major word is listed alphabetically. For example, if one is looking for *criterion test*, it may be found listed as *test, criterion*. Descriptions are incomplete sentences for brevity, with examples and illustrations wherever necessary for clarity. For ease of use the following should be noted: q.v. = which see; /s/ = the sound of s as in sing; *syn.* = synonym. A few words have diacritical markings where the authors felt they were needed. The footnotes indicate a single unique reference or an original use of the term. A few drugs are listed, some with typical dosages, so that, if a report from a physician is read, it can be intelligently understood in the light of other diagnostic findings. Entries are in boldface type for quick identification.

Selection of Terms

The choice of entry terms was arbitrary and based solely on the opinions and experience of the authors. Meanings for the entries are meant to be representative and reflect usage, and they are not meant to be encyclopedic. Selected specific tests with pertinent information about each may be found classified as to type in the appendix. Also in the appendix are the ERIC Clearinghouses and a directory of selected major publishers and distributors as sources of materials. The entries from the related disciplines are those which appear in the reading and learning disabilities literature—textbooks, journals, clinic reports, and so forth.

Acknowledgments

The authors wish to express their appreciation to Lynn and Lori Andrews for their dedication in reviewing entries for duplication and clarity of definition.

Clifford L. Bush, Ed.D.

and

Robert C. Andrews, M.A.

Aa

ability: potential or actual power to perform a responsive act

ability grouping: see grouping, ability

ability, reading: an individual's capacity to interpret printed language symbols rapidly and accurately

abnormal: condition of deviating from the average or expected

abridged edition: reduced form of a book, leaving out some of the detail and retaining major aspects of the original; shortened form of a dictionary by leaving out some of the lesser used words

abstract: brief summary giving the essential points of a book or other communications media; symbolic, opposite of concrete

abstract abilities: individual's capacity to comprehend complex relationships and to react to theoretical considerations

academic (scholastic) aptitude: prediction of success in educational activities usually based upon an index of intelligence and achievement

academic program: content subjects which make up the core of the educational program: history, English, mathematics, etc.

acalculia: inability or loss of the ability to manipulate arithmetic symbols and do mathematical calculations

acceleration: a developmental rate exceeding the normal; promotion of a student in excess of the usual one grade per year; provision in the educational program for advanced learning experiences based on the student's ability rather than grade designation

accelerator: see pacer

accent: to give stress or prominence to a syllable or word

accent, primary: syllable receiving main emphasis in the pronunciation of a given word

accent, secondary: stress weaker than the primary accent and one falling upon a different syllable of a given word

accession: book or other material acquired by a library

accommodation: act of adjusting the lens of the eye to keep a sharply focused image on the retina

acetylcholine (ACH): the chemical agent of transmission at certain synapses; a neurotransmitter

achievement: in the academic sense, progress made by the learner as measured by a test

achievement age (AA): see age, educational

achievement battery: collection of subject-matter standardized tests

achievement quotient (AQ): see quotient, achievement

achromate: a color-blind person

acoustics: science of sound; the relative ease of hearing sound in a room

acquired behavior: individual reactive response to the environment attributed to experience

acronym: word formed from the initial letters of a name, as ERIC (q.v.)

acting out: overt expression of unconscious feeling

acuity: efficiency of response of a sense organ

acuity, auditory: level of hearing sensitivity; keenness of hearing

acuity, visual: ability to distinguish small spatial intervals in the visual field; sharpness, clarity

acute situational or stress reaction: acute emotional reaction relating to extreme environmental stress

adaptation: act of conforming; adjusting one thing to another

addenda: material adding to the completeness of a book but less extensive than a supplement, generally found at the back of the book

adjustment: process in which an individual selects and adapts modes of behavior bringing about a more satisfactory relationship with his environment; educationally, an influential factor in learning

2

adjustment inventory: see inventory, adjustment

adrenalin: extract from the adrenal gland which furnishes sudden stimulation to movement and action; *syn.,* epinephrine

affect: general feeling or emotion

affective: pertaining to emotions, attitudes, and feelings of a learner toward a task; something that arouses emotions

affective domain: the classification of functions by the individual involving emotions and feeling

afferent: nerve conveying impulses toward the nerve center

affix: letter or syllable at the beginning or end of word, which changes the meaning; for example, the *dis* in *dislike* and *ness* in *fullness*

afterimage : persistent effects of stimulation following the withdrawal of the visual stimulus

age, achievement (AA): see age, educational

age, anatomical: system of age assignment based on the relationship between skeletal maturation and chronological age of the average child

age, basal: on a standardized test, the highest age level at which an individual is able to answer correctly all the items

age, carpal: the degree of maturational development of the wrist bones as found in the average child at a given chronological age

age, developmental: measure of development stated in age equivalents

age, educational (EA): level of ability of a student, especially in school work, measured in terms of the average for a given age group, as—if a given score on an achievement test corresponds to an achievement age of 8 years, 4 months—pupils 8 years, 4 months, on the average, will earn this score

age, entrance: minimum chronological age at which a child is allowed to enroll in school

age, equivalent: see norm, age

age-grade table: see table, age-grade

age, grip: age in years and/or months representing an individual's maturity of grip

age, height: age in years and/or months representing an individual's height in relation to the norm

age, mental (MA): performance on a test of mental ability which is typical of a given chronological age

age, norm: see norm, age

age, organismic: average of the measurements of a child's development, scored in age equivalents, including mental, carpal, dental, height, weight, educational and social age

age, reading: level of reading ability in terms of age, based on norms from a reading test, as a score of 8-0 representing a reading age of 8 years, 0 months regardless of chronological age

age, weight : expression of a child's weight in years and months as it falls on a norm age-weight scale

aggression: action carried out forcefully; form of attack may be verbal, physical, or symbolic

agitation: state of chronic restlessness

agitographia: writing dysfunction, as omissions and distortions of letters and words

agnosia: malfunctioning of input sensory channels although the organ is not impaired; due to impairment of the central nervous system, as auditory agnosia, auditory-verbal agnosia, geometric-form agnosia, picture agnosia, tactile agnosia, tactile-verbal agnosia, and visual agnosia

agraphia: type of aphasia associated with a lesion of the central nervous system characterized by inability to recall the kinesthetic patterns that go into writing

air conduction: sound reaches auditory sense organ by traveling through air, through external ear to eardrum and cochlea

albinism: condition characterized by the absence of normal pigmentation, sometimes associated with photophobin, nystagmus, and reduced activity

alexia: inability to interpret written symbols; severe reading disability often the result of brain dysfunction

algorithm: general rule or method of action

allomorph: any of the variant forms of a morpheme; endings of *logs, mats,* and *watches* all have "plural" meaning, but they are dissimilar phonemically (/z/, /s/, /ez/)

allophone: all the members of one phoneme class, e.g., the initial sound

4

of *pill* /p/ and the second sound of *spill* /p/ are phonetically different; they do not indicate a change in meaning even though there is a positional variant

almanac: yearbook of statistics and facts, containing calendar and related events

alpha wave: most common wave form of the EEG from the adult cortex; smooth, regular wave at a frequency of 8-12 cycles per second when at rest

alphabet: system of written characters for a language; generally there is a correspondence between the symbol and speech sound

alphabet, augmented Roman: 44-letter alphabet evolved in England by Sir James Pitman; employs all letters of English alphabet except x and g plus 20 new symbols; each of the 44 letters in the new alphabet stands for only one sound; incorporated in a beginning reading program known as the i.t.a.

alphabet, phonetic: a set of letters and symbols corresponding to speech sounds

alphabetic-classed filing system: grouping of materials into broad subjects alphabetically arranged and also subdivided topically and arranged alphabetically within each class

alternate forms: see forms, equivalent

alternating strabismus: see strabismus, alternating

alternating vision: see vision, alternating

ambidextrous: skilled use of both hands

ambieyedness: condition in which dominance of one eye is lacking

ambiocular: condition (strabismus) in which either eye may be used; lack of fusion though both eyes are functioning

ambivalence: presence of mutually conflicting emotions toward a given person, object, or idea

amblyopia: dimness of sight without any apparent organic defect; not correctable by lenses

amentia: mental deficiency; lack of mental development such as that of idiots and imbeciles

americana: all material of historical significance that has been printed in or about the Americas

ametropia: abnormal condition of the eye resulting in faulty refraction of light rays, as in astigmatism

amusia: inability to use music symbols, both in writing and listening; dysmusia

anaclisis: dependence upon others; as infant and mother

anagrams: word game in which an individual forms a word or phrase by reordering letters of another word or phrase

analogy: a form of logic or reasoning which infers that, if conditions are alike in some respects, they may be alike in other respects

analysis: separation of the whole into its component parts, and perception of their logical relationships

analysis, structural: visual survey of a printed word to determine its pronunciation through the identification of its meaningful (morpheme) parts-roots and affixes, as in *sub-contract-ing*

analysis, word: the use of context, phonic, and structural analysis to identify the sounds and meaning of an unknown word

analytical method: see method, analytical

anarthria: inability to form words accurately due to brain lesion or injury to peripheral nerves which transmit impulses to the articulatory muscles

anatomical age: see age, anatomical

anecdotal records: see records, anecdotal

angular gyrus: see gyrus, angular

aniseikonia: ocular defect in which retinal images do not fuse due to differences in shape and size of the retinal images

anisometropia: a difference in the refractive ability of the eyes

annotation: added note to a bibliography or catalog that describes or evaluates the entry

anomaly: an abnormality; differing from the rule or norm

anomia: inability to recall words or names of objects

anoxia: deficiency in oxygen supply to the brain;or lack of utilization of oxygen by body tissues; brain damage can occur at birth due to orygen deficiency during the transition from maternal supply to the neonate's independent breathing

anthology: collection of the literary works of various authors in one volume or more

anticipatory response: ability to predict probable outcome(s) through logical reasoning; a partial response made when full movement is inhibited; response made before the appropriate stimulus is received

antitropic: mirrored

antonym: word which has the opposite meaning of another; hot is the antonym of cold

anxiety: distressed or apprehensive state of being, often transferred to a situation or object

apathy: indifference; displaying lack of interest or emotion

aphasia: loss or impairment of ability to use or understand language, associated with brain injury

aphasia, expressive: lack of ability to communicate orally

aphasia, receptive: inability to communicate aurally

aphonia: inability to speak, caused by organic psychic disorder

appendix: related material added to a book that is not essential in the body: notes, tables, bibliography, representative samples of forms, list of publishers

apperception: relating of past experience to new knowledge or experiences

apperceptive mass: see background, experiential

application: use of newly learned skills in solving problems or doing school work

apprehension: level of comprehension that is below the mastery level; the fear of a potential future happening

apraxia: difficulty in performing purposeful motor output, in the absence of paralysis or sensory limitation, due to brain lesion or dysfunction

apraxia, constructional: inability to use tools or materials in performing purposeful movements

aptitude, scholastic: see test, scholastic aptitude

aptitudes: native and acquired characteristics that indicate a capacity for future success in learning

aqueous humor: see humor, aqueous

archives: collection of records of a governmental body or organization

arithmetic mean: see mean, arithmetic

arithmetic process: various forms of computation such as adding and subtracting

arithmetic reasoning: application of mathematical processes and computation to solve problems

art therapy: see therapy, art

articulated tests: series of tests in which different levels are utilized for different ages or grades and which have been constructed and standardized so comparable elements can be measured in the overlapping ranges among the test levels; these tests overlap from level to level to allow for the evaluation of the wide range of abilities in a given grade; such a test series yields the same derived scores for a specific grade when either the lower or higher test level is utilized

articulation: ability to produce the sounds of speech; the sequential or continuous development of the school curriculum; the development of different forms and levels of a test that yield comparable results

articulator: movable speech organ: tongue or lips

A-span: abbreviation for eye-voice span

ascenders: those letters which project above the base configuration of the word; in *book,* the *b* and *k* are ascenders

ascending letter: see letter, ascending

aspect: marking of a verb to indicate whether an action is beginning, in progress, completed, repetitive, and so on, as the progressive aspect of *They are racing*

aspirate: breathed sound such as the /*h*/ in *hand*

aspiration: puff of air accompanying the release of a consonant, as with the initial consonants of English *pill* and *kill*

assessment: administration of a test to check the student's mastery of a skill as stated in the performance objective; an evaluation at any aspect or educational function

association: coordination or relationship between ideas and emotions, free or induced

associative learning: see learning, associative

associative learning test: see test, associative learning

astereognosis: form of agnosia in which one cannot recognize objects or their forms by touching them

astigmatism: faulty vision due to irregularity in the curvature of refractive surfaces of the eye

astigmatism, hyperopic: faulty vision due to both hyperopia and astigmatism

asymbolia: loss of ability to understand symbols, such as those used in mathematics and chemistry

asyndetic: describes a catalog without cross-reference

ataxia: lack of coordination in the movement of the voluntary musculature

athetosis: uncontrolled muscular movement marked by slow weaving movement of arms and legs and facial grimaces, due mainly to brain lesion

attention: a set or attitude which makes it possible for the individual to respond precisely to a stimulus; attending or taking notice

attention span: duration of time an individual can attend to a specific task

attitude: set of disposition or opinion involving expectancy of a certain response or happening; a temperament or personality trait

atypical: not conforming to the mode or usual type

auction catalog: listing of books or other objects from private collections offered for sale at auction

audience reading: see reading, audience

audile: person who recalls what he has heard more readily than what he has seen; auditory modality

auding: reception and comprehension of spoken language

audiogram: graphic record showing the audiometer test results of a person hearing, measured in decibels at specific frequencies

audiometer: device for testing hearing acuity and pitch

audio-visual materials: see materials, audio-visual

auditory: relating to hearing

auditory acuity: see acuity, auditory

auditory agnosia: see agnosia

auditory association: auditory vocal association; relationship between words and their meanings

auditory awareness: ability to recognize that a sound has changed, stopped or started

auditory blending: ability to synthesize from left to right the phonemes of a word when they are pronounced separately, thus producing a recognizable word, as /s/, /a/, /t/ = *sat*

auditory closure: task in which a word or sentence must be completed by filling in certain parts (sounds or words) that were omitted when spoken by the teacher

auditory decoding: ability to comprehend spoken words and sounds; auditory comprehension

auditory defect: an imperfection of hearing

auditory discrimination: see discrimination, auditory

auditory figure ground: ability of a child to focus on the essential sound elements and suppress the nonessential noises

auditory focus: ability to localize the source of a sound

auditory imagery: a mental reconstruction of sensory experiences as the result of listening

auditory memory: see memory, auditory

auditory nerve: connection between ear and brain; vibrations of the basilar membranes cause stimulation of the auditory fibers and thus electrochemical impulses are sent to the brain

auditory reception: auditory decoding; understanding words spoken by another person

auditory scanning: ability to relate a present situation to previous auditory experiences

auditory sequencing: ability to recall previously heard details in their correct order

auditory threshold: see acuity, auditory

auditory-vocal association: ability to intelligently respond verbally to a stimulus which has been heard

aura: sensations (such as of flashing or whirling lights) which an epileptic may experience immediately preceding a convulsion; a premonitory subjective feeling

aural: learning through listening; attending with the ears

auricle: the external ear

author card: see card, author

autism, infantile: psychiatric disorder in infants and children with severe disturbance of the ability to communicate in social interaction; children live in their private or autistic mental world

autistic: thought being controlled by the individual rather than by reality: daydreaming, introversion

autistic thinking: mental activity controlled by the individual—wishful thinking or fantasy, as opposed to reality

autograph: signature in the author's own handwriting

auto-instructional methods: see methods, auto-instructional

automatic closure: incidental acquiring of environmental subtleties, as children without instruction developing the syntax of their language

automatic promotion: promotion from one grade to the next regardless of academic achievement; social promotion

autonomic nervous system: sympathetic and parasympathetic nervous systems which control glands and smooth muscles, regulate homeostasis, and contribute to emotional behavior

autonym: a person's real name

auxiliary: verb that combines with another to form a phrase, as *has* in *has been* and *did* in *did go*

average: measure of central tendency; mean, or the sum of the scores divided by the number of scores

axon: structural part of the neuron which transmits impulses away from the cell

Bb

Babinski: extension of the toes, instead of flexion, upon gentle stroking of the sole of the foot, which is normally evident during infancy, but later is a symptom of cerebrospinal disorder (the extensor-plantar response)

backed: sound produced farther back in the mouth than the normal basic position of the sound, as the /c/ of *cool* is backed compared to the /c/ of *calm*

background: one's total experience and education

background, experiential: one's cultural heritage that gives meaning to reading and the various media of instruction; apperceptive mass

balance and rhythm: ability to maintain motor balance and to move rhythmically as an evidence of readiness for perceptual-motor experiences

balanced reading program: see program, balanced reading

bar graph: chart made up of equal-width bars in which the length of the bars represents the level of scores or frequencies

bar reader: device used for training of simultaneous binocular vision through the use of bars between the book page and the reader so that different parts of the page are occluded from the reader's eyes

basal age: see age, basal

basal metabolism: see metabolism, basal

basal reader: graded series of textbooks moving from single to complex skills, which provide the learning and practice to become an independent reader; usually provided for the teacher's use are guides for instruction, workbooks for development of student's skills, and other supplemental aids

basal reader approach: teaching of reading through the use of a series of graded reading textbooks; skills, content, vocabulary are placed in developmental sequence; teachers's manuals and children's workbooks usually accompany the basal readers to guide and reinforce learnings

basal reading: directed reading period wherein the teacher conducts a developmental lesson using the basal reader text

basal-reading program: see program, basal-reading

basal series: graded set of reading texts

basal text: one of a series of basal reader texts

base word: any word conveying meaning which cannot be subdivided into meaningful elements, and to which one or more prefixes or suffixes can be added, also known as stem or root

basic education: subject matter areas that transmit knowledge from the past: English, mathematics, science and social sciences

basic English: simplified, restricted English vocabulary, an international auxiliary language for use in teaching English

basic reader: see basal reader

basic reader vocabulary: see vocabulary, basal-reading

basic sight vocabulary: see vocabulary, basic sight

basic sight words: words immediately recognized without having to analyze them

basic skills: fundamental learning proficiency in reading, writing, computation

basic vocabulary: see vocabulary, basic

battledore: hornbook; early form of primer made from folded paper

behavior: action of the individual considered as a unit

behavior modification: technique for changing human behavior through careful observation of events preceding and following the behavior, based on the theory of operant behavior and conditioning (q.v.)

behavior, overt: observable behavior of an individual

13

behavioral objectives: instructional goals—what the learner will do or accomplish

Benadryl (diphenhydramine): minor tranquilizer or antihistamine which is used to treat emotionally disturbed children, especially those under 12 years; convulsive seizures may be precipitated by large dosages; typical dosage including adult range: 25-400 mg daily

beta wave: brain wave pattern with a frequency of 18-30 cycles per second associated with alertness

bibliophile: lover of books

bibliotherapy: reading material selected for its therapeutic effect on the child, who identifies with its plot and/or characters; initially proposed for maladjusted children

bihemispheric: in the two hemispheres of the brain

bilabial: the sound articulated with both lips, $/b/$, $/m/$, $/p/$

bilateral: occurring on both sides of the body; the use of both sides of the body in parallel fashion

bilingualism: speaking of two languages

bi-modal distribution: frequency distribution with the scores concentrated in two regions and thus resulting in two modes

binaural: hearing with both ears operating together

binding: producing a volume from leaves, sheets, signatures; combining into one volume different issues of periodicals; the cover of a book

binocular: use of both eyes functioning in focus

binocular difficulties: visual impairment in which the eyes do not function together

binocular vision: see vision, binocular

biography: individual's life history

birth trauma: birth injuries such as anoxia and mechanical injury; anxiety or fear symbolically expressed and related back to injury to the psyche at birth

bleed: illustration in a book that runs off the page leaving no margin

blend: the combining of two or three consonants whereby each retains its original sound value, the $/st/$ in *steeple*

blending: technique wherein the child sounds out the phonemic values for the grapheme read in a left-to-right progression, thus correctly pronouncing the word

blind spot: spot on the retina where the optic nerve enters the eye

blockage: desired behavior cannot be achieved by the learner

blocking: sudden inability to recall or communicate or perform a response

blocking, emotional: inability to think or communicate, usually due to the emotion of fear or anger

body abstraction: ability to transfer and generalize self-concepts and location of body parts

body image: complete awareness of one's own body and its shape with its possibilities of movement and performance

body localization: ability to locate the various parts of one's body

body of a book: see book, body of a

body schema: overall pattern of one's sensory awareness of one's body

body size: size of type from top to bottom of the letter; printer's type

body-spatial organization: ability to move in an organized fashion around and through objects in the spatial environment

boldface: type with lines broader than normal so that the words stand out from the rest of the print

bone conduction: transmission of sound to auditory receptors by traveling through bones of skull directly to cochlea

book, body of a: main part of a book

book fair: exhibit of books to arouse interest in reading and books

book jacket: wrapper to cover a book for protection during use

booklet: pamphlet or small book in paper cover

bookmobile: truck or van that takes books to the schools or public in the form of a traveling library

book number: combination of letters and figures to arrange books within the same classification number in alphabetical order

book, picture: book consisting mainly of pictures with simple text

bookrest: device which holds reading material at the appropriate perpendicular angle to the line of sight

books, juvenile: books appropriate to the reading abilities, interests, and tastes of juveniles

books, reference: publications which are consulted to identify facts or background information, e.g., atlas, dictionary, encyclopedia

book, talking: book that has been recorded on record or tape

book week: week in November especially assigned to celebrations and exhibits by booksellers, librarians, and schools to stimulate interest in books and in reading

borderline intelligence: person with an IQ roughly between 70 and 80 (on the Slosson or WISC), which generally suggests placement in a slow learner or retarded class

bowdlerize: to revise a book by deleting or changing objectionable passages

brackets: symbols used to enclose phonetic notation: [ ]

braille: system of printing made up of positioned raised dots for reading by the blind

brain damage: a structural injury to the brain from accident, disease, or surgery

brain-injured child: one who has suffered brain damage before, during, or after birth which may interfere with normal learning or motor functions

brĕve: diacritical mark placed over a vowel to indicate the short sound in pronunciation, *căt*

brochure: brief printed pamphlet

broken home: household in which only one parent is remaining, as disrupted family, broken family

buckram: stiff, heavy book cloth made from cotton

bulletin: numbered publication of a department of government or an institution, usually issued at regular intervals

Cc

cadence: language rhythm

Caldecott Award: annual American Library Association award presented to outstanding artist in illustration of children's books

calendar: a system of reckoning time; a tabular arrangement of days of the week, month, and year; a register indicating chronological order of clinic appointments or court cases

call number: classification system of letters, numbers, and figures placed on the spine of books indicating their specific category and shelf location

calligraphy: art of ornate writing

capability: ability or quality that can be developed or used

capacity: potential point at which learning ceases; set by the limits of the learner's intelligence and psychomotor functioning

capacity level: maximum level at which the individual can comprehend material presented orally

capacity, vital: after inhalation, the greatest amount of air that can be exhaled

caption: title or heading

card, author: catalog card filed under the author's name

card catalog: file composed of individual card entries for each book or source in the library collection

card, main: library's full catalog entry, which gives all the information necessary for complete identification of a work; a master card

card, subject: catalog card filed under the subject

carotid artery: main large artery located on either side of the neck

carrel (carrell): cubicle, generally located in a library, for independent study

cartographer: person who prepares maps or charts

case study: diagnostic analysis of an individual's learning performance in order to determine the nature and causes of his disabilities and propose an appropriate remedial program

cassette: magnetic cartridge designed for playing upon insertion in a cassette-type tape player; playing tape time may be from 15 to 120 minutes

catalepsy: condition in which body or extremities remain in any position in which they are placed

catalog, author: alphabetical catalog of author entries

catalog, union: author or subject library catalog of all the books in specific fields, usually established through cooperative effort of libraries within a geographic area

catastrophic response: complete breakdown in learning or other behavior due to expecting a child to perform beyond his present ability or as a result of some threatening situation

catatonia: type of schizophrenia characterized by immobility and rigidity

catharsis: freeing of repressed emotions by recalling a traumatic experience, acting out aggressions, or empathizing with characters in a book or play

causal factors: conditions responsible for academic disabilities which, when remedied, will result in improved performance

causal relationship: comparison of two factors in which the one influences the other; independent and dependent variables

cause, constitutional: due to an organic deficiency rather than familial inheritance

cause, primary: main or most important factor

ceiling: upper limit of ability measured by a test

centile: percentile; per hundred

central nervous system (CNS): brain and spinal cord

central tendency: a score which best represents a given distribution of scores, e.g., mean, median, or mode; the average of a group of scores

central thought: main idea of an oral or written selection

cephalo-caudal principle: theory that development progresses from the head-neck region downward to the lower extremities

cerebral: referring to brain

cerebral cortex: external gray layer of the brain

cerebral dominance, mixed: language disturbance theoretically assigned to confusion of the function of the dominant and non-dominant hemispheres of the cerebrum so that one hemisphere does not always predominate in control of body movements

cerebral localization: locating the relatively small areas of the brain that control certain physiological functions

cerebral palsy: paralysis caused by a lesion in the brain which can be found at birth, resulting in a weakening of the limbs; may include ataxia, involuntary movements and possibly some degree of mental deficiency

cerebrospinal fluid: fluid of the canals of the brain

cerebrum: the brain

cerumen: earwax

cervical adenopathy: enlargement of the lymph nodes of the neck

character disorder: socially disapproved patterns of behavior and emotional response in conjunction with observed anxiety

chart, experience: group-dictated ideas or sentences which the teacher prints on paper or chalkboard, based on children's common experience, used in beginning reading; sometimes used in clinical setting so the child can "read" his own experiences; the experience chart is one element of the language experience approach

chart, progress: graphic record showing progress in vocabulary, speed, comprehension, and other reading skills usually recorded by the reader, used as a motivation for improvement

checked vowel: vowel in a closed syllable (ending in a consonant), as in *set* and *sat*

checklist, diagnostic: list of specific behavioral acts checked by the teacher (diagnostician) to guide instruction

child-centered: academic instruction utilizing the specific needs, interests, and abilities of the pupils

child study team: special service team; group of trained professionals representing psychology, psychiatry, learning disabilities, social work, medical and remedial disciplines charged with the responsibility of identifying, examining, classifying and placing children who meet the critieria of exceptional child as defined by the particular agency

chiroscopic drawing: tracing of an image guided by the eye not receiving the actual visual stimulus

cholinesterase (kō-la-nĕs-tar-ās) (CHE): enzyme reputed to remove acetylcholine at synapses; appears to act as a circuit breaker

choral reading: group reading in unison

chorea: motor disorder characterized by jerky, spasmodic movements

choreiform syndrome: term used by Dutch author Prechtl to describe the symptoms characteristic of children who have reading disabilities, including hyperkinesis, faulty dominance, dyskinesia, visual-perceptual difficulties and poor concentration

choroid: dark brown, vascular layer of the eye, which nourishes the retina and lens and darkens the eye

chromosomal sex: genetic sex revealed by the chromosome count, which is 44+ XX in females and 44+ XY in males

chromosomes: threadlike structures found in nucleus of cells along which are arranged the genes (q.v.); in man there are 22 pairs of autosomes and 1 pair of XY sex chromosomes; in females there are 22 pairs of autosomes and 1 pair of XX sex chromosomes

chronological age: length of time a person has lived; calendar age

chronological age grade placement: scale indicating relationship between chronological age (q.v.) and school grade; each school grade and month has an equivalent chronological age, as grade 3.0 = age 8-0

chunking: arranging adjacent elements into meaningful groups for understanding and recall; i.e., 7743477 chunked as 774-35-77

CIJE (*Current Index to Journals in Education*): contains annotated articles from about 600 educational journals; each article assigned a six-digit EJ (for Educational Journal) accession number

circa: about; precedes a date, as circa 800 B.C.

circumflex: diacritical mark, as *ûrge*

citation: reference to a work from which a passage has been quoted; source of authority

citation form: linguistic form spoken in isolation, as *have* instead of *'ve* in *I could've gone*

class interval: see interval, class

classic: excellent work of literature because it is recognized as outstandingly representative of the finest in its field

classification: the organization of facts into categories based on a logical commonality, such as nouns, verbs, fruits, vegetables

classification, Dewey decimal: Dewey's organization system for book collections using 10 main divisions in a numbered system

000-099	General Works	500-599	Pure Science
100-199	Philosophy	600-699	Applied Science
200-299	Religion	700-799	Fine Arts
300-399	Social Science	800-899	Literature
400-499	Language	900-999	History

classroom library: see library, classroom

Clement's minimal brain dysfunction syndrome: describes a child of average intelligence who exhibits some learning disabilities as a result of a dysfunction of the central nervous system; differentiates major brain disorders such as cerebral palsy and epilepsy from minimal disorders having symptoms such as poor concentration, hyperactivity or perceptual and motor impairment

climate, emotional: overall circumstances affecting emotional response, such as the characteristic condition resulting from the learner interacting with his classroom environment

clinic, reading: place where a team of specialists diagnose reading disabilities, prescribe treatment, and often provide remedial services

clinical diagnosis: see diagnosis, clinical

closed syllable: see syllable, closed

closure: mental process whereby one perceives an incomplete form as though it were complete

cloze procedure: technique used for evaluation of pupil performance and pupil's reading ability level involving the deletion of every fifth word from running context; the learner is expected to complete the thought

clue, configuration: form or shape by which the individual can identify the word

clue, context: using the surrounding phrases or sentences as an aid to word recognition

clue, language rhythm: word recognition technique involving the order or sequence of rhyming words which suggest the potentially correct response

clue, picture: use of illustrations to suggest words and meaning for the accompanying material being read

cluster: two or three consonants or vowels that blend to form a sound which is different from the sound of the individual letters, see digraph and glides

cluttering: speech so rapid that enunciation is distorted, parts of words are omitted, and sounds are substituted

CNS: central nervous system; the brain and spinal cord

cochlea: shell-like cavity of inner ear containing the endings of the auditory nerve and the auditory receptors

code: set of symbols used to represent a system

coefficient of correlation: a statistic indicating the degree of relationship between two sets of measures, ranging from perfect negative (-1.00) to perfect positive (+1.00); does not imply causal relation; (formulae: r indicates Pearson product moment correlation and ρ (rho) indicates Spearman rank order correlation)

coefficient of reliability: correlation coefficient used to indicate a test's consistency or stability; scores on equivalent forms, matched halves, or on two administrations of the same test are correlated

cognition: process of knowing, perceiving, or reasoning

cognitive memory: single reproduction of items remembered from content studies; recall

cognitive process: mental activity in which the individual begins with the concrete level of knowledge and may proceed through the abstract levels of analysis and synthesis

collaborator: person who works with others in writing a book or article

collected works: complete assemblage of an author's works, usually in one volume

collection: an assembly of documents segregated from other record groups to facilitate service or preservation, as a collection of indexes

collocation: the probability that two or more words will occur together, as *plane, air, fly*

colloquial: spoken conversation or writing that is in tune with the local form of grammar

color blindness: total or partial inability to distinguish colors, more common among males

color perception: visual impression of hue; chromatic aspect under normal conditions of illumination

common learnings: experiences gained through normal pedagogical (q.v.) participation

communication: interchange of information or thought by speech, print, signs, or signals; the message which is communicated

compensation: defensive reaction to offset loss of status or some personal deficiency such as inferiority or guilt feelings

compensatory eye movements: see eye movements, compensatory

compiler: one who selects and combines into one work the writings of another author or authors

complementary distribution: variants of a linguistic unit which occur in different environments: /s/ in *cats* and /z/ in *cogs*

complementation: structural relationship between a verb and its complement, as in *ride-the bicycle*

complex sentence: sentence which contains a main thought unit and a subordinated (embedded) thought unit, as *He jumped when I whistled*

component: element in a larger structure

compound phonogram: see phonogram, compound

compound word: combination of two or more elements, each usually a word, which form a new word, as *foot* and *ball* become *football*

comprehension: understanding of the meaning of spoken, written, or nonverbal language

comprehension, critical: type of reading in which the individual, utilizing his entire background of learning experience, evaluates the material being read

comprehension, inferential: interpretive understanding; ability to derive meaning that is not specifically stated in the reading; to understand what is only implied

comprehension level: maximum level of understanding from a reading or listening selection; the ability of the individual to understand material received aurally

comprehension, literal: specific meaning of any written or spoken word, regardless of interpretation of the whole (Gestalt); usually literal comprehension as used in reading or listening

comprehension, paragraph: ability to understand the central thought and subordinate ideas in a paragraph

comprehension, rate of: see reading, rate of comprehension

comprehension test: see test, comprehension

comprehension, word: understanding the meaning(s) of a word

compulsion: irresistible urge to perform an act contrary to one's better judgment or will

compulsiveness: insistance on repeatedly performing some behavior in an habitual fashion

concave: possessing a curved, depressed surface; the opposite of convex

concentrated repetition: in psychology, a performance repeated in one sitting, as opposed to distributed repetition

concentration: exclusive persistent focusing on a given task or object

concept: the product of understandings; a mental image; an abstract idea often represented by a word; influenced by experiential background

conceptual background: refers to the generalizations the student has before he begins a new task, such as reading a book

conceptual disorders: disturbance of the cognitive process in thinking activities

conceptual readiness: see readiness, conceptual

conceptualization: thinking process by which the essential elements of a specific situation are abstracted and applied generally to a class as a series of experiences, e.g., different breeds of dogs produce the idea of dogness, which is then applied to new experiences with dogs in general

concordance: index of principal words in the Bible or the works of an author, indicating location in the text

concretism: type of thinking in which the individual approaches each situation as a unique one, unable to recognize similarities

concurrent validity: see validity, concurrent

conditioning, classical: process in which a response to one stimulus comes to be made to a second stimulus as a result of close temporal association between them, e.g., Pavlov's *conditioned reflex* wherein dogs salivated at the sound of a bell that had been previously linked with the presence of food

conditioning, operant or instrumental: process in which a response to a stimulus which is followed by a rewarding stimulus (food or pain relief) is more likely to be made whenever the first stimulus is present, e.g., if a caged rat sees a bar, presses it and receives food, it is more likely to press the bar when the bar is present.

conduction deafness: hearing impairment caused by defective mechanical processes, usually in the middle ear

configuration: general form, shape, and distinctive features of a word

conflict, emotional: frustration caused by the discrepancy between opposing goals or between a goal and the level the individual can actually attain

confusion: lack of orientation in regard to time, place and/or person

confusion in dominance: lack of clear orientation due to crossed dominance (q.v.)

congenital: present at birth, but not necessarily hereditary

congenital word blindness: see word blindness

connotation: an idea generated by a word or phrase, beyond its direct meaning

consonant: single letter sound formed by constriction of the air stream in the vocal tract, as opposed to the vowels; $/w/$ and $/y/$ may act as vowels also; some consonants are silent in certain words

consonant blend: see blend

consonant cluster: sequence of two or more consonants as the $/nd/$ in *sand,* the $/ng/$ in *sing,* and the $/tch/$ in *catch;* blend as $/st/$, $/sk/$, $/cl/$, $/dr/$, $/sm/$

consonant digraph: see digraph, consonant

consonant, final: one at the end of a word, as $/t/$ in *cat*

consonant, initial: one at the beginning of a word, as $/c/$ in *cat*

consonant, medial: one appearing within a word, as $/l/$ in *sailor*

consonant substitution: see substitution, consonant

consonant trigraph: three consonants appearing together in a word, as /*tch*/ in *catcher*

consonant, voiced: one produced by the vibraton of the vocal cords, as /*d*/ and /*g*/

consonant, voiceless: one not produced by vocal cord movement, as /*f*/ and /*h*/

consonant-vowel blend: see blend

constituent structure: grammatical construction; combining of elements of speech

constituents: component morphemes of a grammatical construction, as *Joe/cried*

constitutional cause: see cause, constitutional

construct validity: see validity, construct

content subjects: subjects such as history, science, and English which have as a primary objective the acquisition of knowledge

content validity: see validity, content

content words: those words that have a definite referent in the culture, as *car, highway, skyscraper*

context: the words surrounding an unknown word which suggest the meaning or pronunciation of that word; the words composing the reading matter

context clue: see clue, context

contextual analysis: use of the total sentence to get the meaning of a specific unknown word

continuants: consonant or vowel which can be prolonged without change in its quality, as /*f*/ in *cliff*; in contradistinction to a stop (q.v.)

continuity: sequence of learnings wherein each step is dependent upon previous learnings to build toward a total coordinated goal

continuous progress plan: organizational plan in which children are placed on basis of achievement rather than grade or age; movement from one group to another based on readiness; all movement based on mastery

continuous variable: value which can assume any point or level on the scale, as *test scores, time, distance,* as opposed to a *discrete variable*

contraction: short form for two words which often appear together, as *we have* becomes *we've*

contralateral: action in unison with the counterpart on the opposite side of the body

control: procedure in an experimental design in which the experimental variable is absent, but all other conditions are the same; experimental and control groups have all factors in common except the one variable in the experimental groups; thus, differences can be ascribed to the experimental variable

controlled reader: an adapted filmstrip projector which presents material at adjustable rates

controlled vocabulary: see vocabulary, controlled

convergence: axes of the two eyes are turned inward to focus the image on the retina when sighting at varying distances

convergent strabismus: crossed eyes

convergent thinking: analysis of given data, which because of its structured nature produces a single correct answer to the problem; opposite of divergent thinking

converted score: see score, converted

convex: surface that is curved and elevated at the center; opposite of concave

Cooper method: VAKT system (q.v.) which modified Fernald's approach by having the child write the words in a shallow tray of sand or salt; reading in print is avoided until the child has learned the vocabulary of three pre-primers

coordination: structural relationship between two grammatical units joined by *and, but, or,* as in *salt and pepper* and *short but sweet;* the relationship between two parts of the body, as eye and hand

coordination, eye-hand: harmonious use of the muscles of the eyes and the hands in cooperative effort

copyright: exclusive legal right to publish and control a literary, musical, or artistic work for a given number of years

core: essential elements as the key skills and procedures in a specific content; type of program with a group of very closely related courses considered to be the core, central focus of the instruction

cornea: transparent membrane covering the outer layer of the eyeball

correction-for-guessing formula: formula sometimes used in scoring objective tests to make allowance for guessing, as:

$R-W, R-\dfrac{W}{A-1}$, where R = Rights, W = Wrongs and A = number of alternate choices per each item

corrective reading: see reading, corrective

corrective teaching: special instruction given to an individual based on the diagnosis of a delimited weakness; usually done by the classroom teacher because the student's needs are apparently not serious enough for clinical remediation

correlation: degree of relationship between two variables, ranging from -1.00 perfect negative relationship to +1.00 perfect positive; expressed as coefficient of correlation, r for product moment and ρ (rho) for rank order correlation. No causal relationship is assumed

cortex, cerebral: the outer layer of the cerebrum

cranial nerves: nerves arising within the cranium, such as the optic and auditory nerves

creative reading: integrating and organizing reading materials in order to come to some conclusion or synthesis, or to solve a problem

cretinism: stunting of physical and mental growth due to thyroid deficiency, appearing in early childhood

criterion: standard used as a basis for qualitative or quantitative comparison; grade point average is a criterion on which to judge a predictive test

criterion-keying: process of constructing a test's scoring key empirically by observing characteristic differences in answers provided by different persons

criterion level: number of correct items on test a student must achieve as indication of skill mastery

criterion test: see test, criterion

critical comprehension: see comprehension, critical

critical period: period in life history which is crucial to continued maximum growth and maturation in a particular area; if this period is not capitalized upon, the individual may never achieve maximum growth in that area

critical ratio (CR): ratio of the difference between two means to the standard error of the difference, a test of significance of differences

critical reading: see reading, critical

critical thinking: making a judgment, value, or choice

crossed dominance: sensorimotor functioning in which the preferred side of the body differs for hands and eyes, e g , individual is right-handed and left-eyed, or left-handed and right-eyed

cross-extension pattern: characteristic arm-leg pattern observed in natural walking, creeping, or crawling consisting of concurrent movement of the front of the arm and leg on opposite body side

crossing the midline: movement across the midsection of the body without involvement of any other body part, as a hand and forearm or foot and leg

cross-lateral coordination: working together of body parts on the opposite sides of the body

cross-modality perception: the neurological process which converts information received through one modality to another system within the brain; also referred to as intersensory transfer

cross-validation: process of verifying results obtained on one group by replication with a second, comparable group

crystalline lens: transparent, convex lens in the eye just behind the pupil

C-score: normalized standard score (q.v.) of eleven units; with mean = 5.5, standard deviation = 2

cue: stimulus; object that causes action, as pictures provide additional meaning in a story

cultural level: enlightenment and refinement acquired through intellectual and esthetic training

cultural reading: see reading, cultural

culture: pattern of living associated with a specific society

culture-free test: instrument devised to cancel the effects of an individual's previous environment on his score; actually this is not as yet fully possible in a pencil-and-paper test

cumulative index: index reference updating with latest articles, previous indexes

curriculum: the sum of courses and experiences provided for the learner by a given school

curriculum validity: see content validity

cursive writing: see writing, cursive

cursory reading: see reading, cursory

curve, normal: symmetrical, bell-shaped curve of a normal distribution of scores (q.v.)

cyanosis: bluish appearance of the skin due to lack of oxygen in the blood as a result of poor circulation, delayed or inadequate breathing

cybernetics: interaction between people and machines or instruments of their environment

cyclophoria: rotation of the eyeball due to imbalance of the musculature of the eyes

cylert: a non-amphetamine drug used to treat hyperactivity in children

cytoarchitectonic: referring to cellular structure of a region, as tissue or organ

Dd

data (plural of datum): group of facts

db: see decibel

deafened: individual who, after acquiring some facilities in speech and listening comprehension, suffers a hearing loss

deafness, nerve: deafness resulting from lesions associated with sensory receptors of the cochlea or acoustic nerve fibers

Deanol: mild antidepressant drug utilized with children who have learning disabilities; reports on its effectiveness on hyperkinetic behavior are controversial; side effects include twitching, constipation, rashes, insomnia and muscular tension; dosages include adult range, 25-300 mg daily

decibel: unit used for expressing intensity of sound

decile: one of nine points which divide a ranked distribution into 10 parts of equal frequency; the first decile is the 10th percentile, the fifth decile the 50th percentile, and the 9th decile the 90th percentile

decile rank: derived score expressed in terms of the nearest decile; a decile rank of 1 is given to any value between the first and ninth percentiles inclusively

decimal classification: see classification, Dewey decimal

decode: ability to identify sound value (phoneme) of the printed symbol (grapheme); being able to look at the printed symbol *cart* and pronounce the word *cart*

dedication: author's statement preceding a work showing his appreciation, indebtedness, or recognition for aid or use of material

deduction: reasoning process in which a conclusion is drawn from the logic of the situation; also the conclusion itself

deductive: reasoning process involving application of a generalization to specific situation

deep structure: abstract structure theorized as underlying a sentence containing all necessary information for semantic interpretation of that sentence

deep subject: noun phrase that is the subject of a deep structure and that may or may not become the surface subject, as Paul kicked Harry and Harry was kicked by Paul; Paul is the deep subject of both sentences but only the surface subject of the first sentence

defect: absence of a necessary component for completeness, adequacy, or perfection

defect, ocular: physical or mechanical dysfunction of the eye that interferes with the normal operation of the visual system

defense mechanism: behavioral characteristic utilized by an individual for protection against anxiety-producing conditions

deficiency, mental: term encompassing all the levels below normal intelligence

deficit modality instruction: procedure seeking to improve performance in the weakest modality by making it productive for learning

deictic word: "pointing" or demonstrative word, such as *those, them, there, that*

delayed speech: see speech, delayed

delinquent: individual, usually a minor, who is a criminal or social offender; failing in a duty or obligation

delta wave: brain wave with a frequency between .5-3.5 cycles per second; found normally during sleep, but if found in an awake adult is suggestive of pathology

delusion: false belief that reason cannot correct

demography: study of vital statistics related to human populations

dendrite: part of neuron's structure which receives nerve impulses

denial: unconscious defense mechanism used in allaying anxiety and resolving conflicts by refusing to admit existence of anxiety-causing objects

denotation: exact meaning of a word as found in a dictionary

dentals: sounds formed by pressing the tip of tongue against the teeth /t/, /d/

departmentalized schools: organizational pattern in which specific teachers are assigned to instruct their particular subject specialties

depression: morbid, unrealistic sadness contrasted to grief which is realistic; varies in depth from neurosis to psychosis

depth perception: see perception, depth

derivative: word composed of a root plus one or more formative elements called affixes, such as in *repay, payable, repayable*

derived score: see score, derived

derived sentence: any sentence developed by utilizing transformation principles applied to the basic sentence

descending letter: letter which extends below the line of printing, as *p, q, g*

deterioration: progressive intellectual and/or emotional disintegration, as in psychoses

determiner: word preceding a noun signalling that a noun is following; may be used in place of nouns as substitutes

development: changes in the organism from conception to death

developmental age: see age, developmental

developmental programs: arrangement of learning designs which considers the normal growth and development patterns of children

developmental reading: see reading, developmental

developmental reading period: instructional lesson in which groups are given directed learning in specific aspects of the basal program

developmental sequences of tasks: ordered series of tasks from simple to complex

deviant or nonsense sentence: sentence that poses a comprehension difficulty to native speaker due to its semantic unusualness: *Cows laughed purple circles*

deviation: in statistics, the amount of difference between a score and a specific reference point, usually the mean

deviation, average: in a frequency distribution, the average amount of difference between the scores and the mean

deviation IQ: normed standard score on an intelligence test; the student's raw score is compared to his age group with the average score adjusted to 100 and the standard deviation set at 15 or 16

deviation, quartile (Q): measure of variability, half the difference between the first quarter (25th percentile) and the third quarter (75th percentile) scores

deviation, standard: see standard deviation

Dewey decimal classification: see classification, Dewey decimal

Dexedrine (dextroamphetamine sulfate): central nervous system or psychotropic (q.v.) drug used to treat learning disabled children; increases attention span; dosage for children varies from 2.5 to 20 mg, 2 to 3 times per day; can depress appetite

dextrad: pertaining to the right side; progressing from left to right

dextral: pertaining to the right side; right-handed

dextrality: tendency toward use of right hand or right side

diacritical mark: system of signs or characters employed as indicators of specific sound values for a letter or group of letters

diagnosis: analysis of available information, subjective and objective, to determine the nature, etiology and pattern of a disability; such activity has as its goal the development of a prescriptive program for correction

diagnosis, clinical: intensive analysis of person's disability made by a specialist or team of specialists representing various disciplines; in current practice a prescriptive program is incorporated

diagnosis, learning disability: thorough analysis and description of a learning disability; its purpose is to identify the problem, to locate etiology and prescribe remedial and corrective steps; generally part of a larger child study clinical diagnosis

diagnosis, reading: thorough analysis and description of a reading disability; its purpose is to identify the reader's difficulties, to locate etiology and prescribe remedial and corrective treatment (the latter task is assumed in current practice)

diagnostic checklist: see checklist, diagnostic

diagnostic outcome assessments: identification of weaknesses and strengths in student performance on a specific skill group related to a competence area

diagnostic prescriptive teaching: instructional process involving pre-evaluation, analysis of need, selection of objective structuring of learning environment, teaching, reinforcement, post-evaluation

diagnostic test: see test, diagnostic

dialect: variation of a spoken language found in specific area or social group; the differences can occur in pronunciation, vocabulary, and grammatical condition

diction: style of oral expression or choice of words to indicate meaning; enunciation

dictionary, picture: dictionary of words with pictures illustrating the entries

dictionary skills: see skills, dictionary

differences, individual: degree to which an individual is unlike comparable individuals; some common variables are intelligence, specific skill areas, physical and emotional characteristics

differential meaning: meaning difference that must occur when two statements are not repetitions; *he shot a deer* and *he shot a rabbit* indicate differential meaning

differentiated instruction: see instruction, differentiated

differentiation: ability to use different parts of the body independently in a specific and controlled way, such as the ability to stimulate the muscles in one leg without doing the same to any other body part not required in executing the task

difficulty value: statistical term indicating the degree of difficulty for a specific test item; it is usually expressed as a percentage of the group answering correctly

digest: brief resumé of a written work; shortened articles from longer ones or from a book

digraph: group of successive letters whose phonetic value is one sound, as /ee/ in *tree,* or a different value from the individual letters, as /sh/ in *shoe*

digraph, consonant: group of successive consonants whose phonetic value is not the sum of their individual sounds but that of one unique sound; such as /sh/ in *shoe*

digraph, vowel: group of successive vowels whose phonetic value is one sound, as /ee/ in *tree*

Dilantin (diphenylhydantoin): anticonvulsant drug used for epilepsy and hyperactivity in children

diopter: unit of measure for the refracting power of a lens; the distance required by the lens to focus light, divided by one

diphthong: the combining of two vowels so their individual sounds blend producing a new phoneme in which the original sounds are not heard, as /oi/ in *oil*

diplopia: condition in which one object is seen as two; double vision

directed reading activity: developmental reading lesson which includes: background and vocabulary, guided silent reading, purposeful oral re-reading, specific skills instruction, and enrichment activities

directional confusion: characteristic of making reversals and substitutions resulting from a left-right orientation disorder

directionality: ability to distinguish right from left, above from below, in from out, forward from backward, up from down; to establish directional orientation

directory: alphabetical list, sometimes in topical arrangement, of persons, schools, organizations, etc. with data about each

disabled reader: see reader, disabled

discourse: group of sentences related in some manner

discrete value: discontinuous value obtained by counting rather than measuring; only whole number values can be assigned, as number of books in library and number of students in class

discriminating power: degree to which a test item can differentiate between individuals as to their level of ability in a specific area

discrimination: process of detecting similarities and differences between stimuli

discrimination, auditory: ability to detect similarities and differences among sound stimuli

discrimination, word: process of recognizing, pronouncing and associating meaning for specific word configurations

discriminator: specific aspect of a word that serves to distinguish it from other similar words; the part that requires special emphasis by the learner

discriminatory power: see power, discriminatory

disinhibition: inability to restrain oneself from reacting to distracting stimuli

displacement: unconscious defense mechanism in which an emotion is transferred from original object to a more acceptable substitute

dissociation: lack of the ability to perceive things as a whole or as a gestalt; the result is a tendency to respond in terms of parts

dissyllable: word with two syllables, such as *income*

distortion: prime mechanism assisting to repress and camouflage unacceptable thoughts

distractibility: inability to hold one's attention; the tendency to be easily drawn to extraneous stimulus or to focus on unimportant details

distractor: an incorrect alternate in a multiple-choice item

distribution, frequency: organization of scores, generally from high to low, indicating the number of times (frequency) each score occurs

distribution, normal: bell-shaped distribution of scores with an equal number of scores above and below the mean; 68.26% of the scores are found within one standard deviation ± the mean; the frequency distribution obtained with a large number of scores subject to the laws of probability

divergent eye movements: eye movements in which the axes of the eyes turn outward or diverge

divergent thinking: analysis of a problem resulting in multiple solutions or conclusions which an individual may rank in order of value; opposite of convergent thinking

Dolch List: a list of 220 basic words to be recognized at sight, lately revised by Kucera and Francis and others

dominance, cerebral: hemispheric dominance; concept that one side of the brain (hemisphere) generally leads in control of certain body movements

dominance, hand-and-eye: the inclination for the dominant hand and eye to be on the same side

dominance, lateral: condition existing due to preference in use of one side of the body, such as handedness and eyedness

dominance, mixed: theory that some reading or speech disorders may result from confused dominance of the cerebral hemispheres; left-right confusion

double entry: entry in a catalog under two subject headings, as Lakes, New Jersey and New Jersey Lakes

double vision: *syn.,* diplopia

Down's syndrome: condition characterized by a flat skull, slanting eyes, stubby fingers, fissured tongue, and retardation described in 1866 by J. Landen Down; mongolism; associated with an extra chromosome 21

DRA: abbreviation for Directed Reading Activity

drills: systematic repetition of an act to aid in the retention of some specific skill

drive: tendency to be sensitive to certain class stimuli which will result in desire for and attainment of a specific goal

drug therapy: treatment with drugs; medication prescribed for children with learning disabilities in an attempt to increase attention span and decrease hyperactivity

dual standardization: system of standardizing two tests concurrently on one sample, thus integrating the two instruments

dynamic balance: capacity to maintain equilibrium while involved in balancing tasks

dynamic prehensile theory of vision: theory which suggests that the eyes are not passive receivers but actively seek sensory abstraction from the environment

dynamics: determination of how the development of behavior patterns and/or emotional reactions take place

dynamometer: instrument used for measuring strength of grip

dysacusis: impairment in hearing not involving sensitivity loss but rather distortion of loudness and/or pitch

dysarthria: inability to articulate speech sounds intelligibly, reflecting a CNS dysfunction in speech motor musculature

dysbulia: confusion in the ability to think and to attend

dyscalculia: a partial disturbance of the ability to manipulate arithmetic symbols and to do mathematical calculations

dysdiadochokinesis: lack of the ability to perform repetitive movements as finger tapping

dysfunction: abnormal functioning

dysgraphia: inability to perform the required motor tasks for handwriting and, thus the power to express ideas by writing; often a result of brain lesion or dysfunction

dyskinesia: impairment of the power of voluntary movement, resulting in fragmentary and poorly coordinated movement

dyslalia: impaired speech of functional origin or due to defective speech organs

dyslexia: inability to read or to understand what one reads silently or orally; condition generally associated with brain dysfunction

dysnomia: condition characterized by the inability to recall words at will even when the individual knows the word he wishes to recall and can recognize it when said

dysphasia: inability or difficulty in writing or speaking as a result of brain damage or dysfunction; *syn.,* aphasia

dysrhythmia: speech fluency characterized by defective stress, intonation and breath control

Ee

echolalia: dysfunction characterized by the repetition of words or phrases spoken by another; such repetition does not convey meaning

echopraxia: automatic repetition of movements

ecology of behavior: study of the relationship between living organisms and their physical and social environment

edition: all the issues of a work printed from one setting of type

editor: person who collects, reviews, and organizes other authors' materials for publication

EDRS ERIC Document Reproduction Service: source of documents in microfiche (MF) or hard copy (HC) as indexed in RIE (q.v.); when ordering from EDRS, specify quantity, ED number, and kind desired, MF or HC; EDRS address: P.O. Drawer O, Bethesda, Maryland 20014

educable retardate: individual within an IQ range of 50 to 75 as measured by an individualized test of mental ability

educational age (EA): see age, educational

educational guidance: part of the counseling and guidance program

educational measurement: techniques of determining achievement, aptitude and intelligence through a systematic articulated assessment program

educational quotient (EQ): see quotient, educational

educationally handicapped: children with learning problems generally caused by emotional, physical or environmental factors

EEG: see electroencephalogram

efferent: nerve conveying impulses away from the nerve center

efficiency, visual: ability to perform visual tasks comfortably and easily in differing situations

ego: the self as differentiated from others

ego identity: unity and persistence of one's individuality, as experienced in self-awareness and behavior

egocentric: preoccupied with self to the relative exclusion of the concerns of others

eidetic imagery: type of internal visualization in which the stimulus is reproduced as though it were actually there; a primary memory image which is common in childhood but rare in adults

EKG (electrocardiogram): a graphic record of changes in electric potential as the heart contracts and relaxes

elaboration: extension by the addition of variations of associated movements or ideas

electroencephalogram (EEG): graphic record of changes in the electrical potential of the brain over time

electroencephalograph: instrument that is utilized in producing an electroencephalogram

electromyogram: a graphic record of changes in electrical potential during muscle contraction

electrooculogram: an electrographic tracing of eye movements using the for example, the reading eye camera

embedded sentence: sentence that is part of another, as (when) *they played* is embedded in *we cried when they played*

emmetropia: normal refraction of the eye when an object is sharply imaged on the retina

emotion: intensified feeling such as joy, sadness, fear, hate, guilt, love, which is generally accompanied by physiological and psychomotor activities

emotional bias: prejudice resulting from intense feeling

emotional blocking: see blocking, emotional

emotional climate: see climate, emotional

emotional conflict: see conflict, emotional

emotional lability: ambivalent emotional behavior characterized by easy, unexplainable arousal and shift from one emotion to another

emotional maturity: see maturity, emotional

emotional stability: normal and dependable reaction of an individual who does not react excessively to affective (q.v.) stimuli

empathy: intellectual awareness of the feelings of another person

empirical: data gained from direct observation, information, and experimentation

empirical validity: test validity based on data from specific studies which have been carried out substantiating variable in question

empyema: indication of pus in a hollow organ, space, or cavity

encephalitis: acute inflammation of the brain substance or its membranous coverings

encephalography (EEG): examination of the brain by X-ray or electro-encephalograph

encoding: analysis and conversion of oral language into representative written symbols in reading; in general the conversion from one system of communication to another

endings: additions to words, such as *s, es, ed, ied, ing;* words composed of a word and an ending are known as *variants*

endocrine glands: glands which secrete a hormone directly into the bloodstream which acts as a chemical regulator of physiological activity

endocrinology: study dealing with body's internal secretions from whatever source including pituitary, thyroid, adrenal, and sex glands

endogenous: originating within the structure of system; can be hereditary or genetic

endophasia: inner speech without the use of the vocal organs; verbal thinking

engram: altered condition of living tissue associated with memory traces

enrichment: expansion of the educational program at the same instructional level by providing wider learning experiences

entrance age: see age, entrance

entry, main: full catalog entry, usually the author entry, providing the pertinent information needed for a comprehensive identification

entry vocabulary: words listed alphabetically in a dictionary which are defined and marked for pronunciation

enunciation: clear and distinct articulation of words and sounds

enuresis: bed wetting

epigraph: motto or brief quotation introducing a book or a chapter

epilepsy: brain disorder characterized by excessive neuronal discharge, accompanied by temporary episodes of motor, sensory, or psychic dysfunction with or without convulsive movements; during such a seizure or episode there is a marked change in recorded electrical brain activity

epileptogenic foci: areas of the brain, scarred or otherwise injured, that become starting points of epileptic seizures

epitome (e-pit´-o-mē): concise statement of a subject, article, or book

equated scores: derived scores comparable from test to test, as standard scores, grade placements, mental ages, etc.

equivalent forms: see forms, equivalent

ERIC-CRIER: Educational Resources Information Center-Clearinghouse for Retrieval of Information and Evaluation of Reading; acquires, examines, and disseminates research reports, materials, and information related to all aspects of reading; address-National Council of Teachers of English, 1111 Kenyon Road, Urbana, Illinois 61801

ERIC-RCS: Educational Resources Information Center-Reading and Communication Skills; collects, analyzes, evaluates, and disseminates educational information related to research, instruction, and personal preparation at all levels, and in all institutions, concerned with instruction in reading, English, journalism, speech, and theater; address-1111 Kenyon Road, Urbana, Illinois 61801

erotica: literature with sexual love or desire as its theme

errata: listing or printing of typographical errors in a specific work with their corrections

error: in testing, a generic term for those elements in a test which function to keep the test from yielding valid results; a wrong response; a negative force in learning as opposed to successes

errors, random: effect on a set of scores of chance variables such as guessing or anxiety, etc.

errors, systematic: errors that consistently affect all measures in the same direction, introducing a systematic bias into the series, as constant error

esophoria: see esotropia

esotropia: crossed eyes

essay test: see test, essay

etiology: study of the causes of a dysfunction

etymology: study of the origin, history, and derivation of words

euphony: agreeableness of sound and ease of pronunciation

euphoria: mood or emotional attitude of health and well-being; elation

evaluation: in education, a process of determining the effectiveness of instruction for an individual, a group, or a whole program, examining subjective judgment, qualitative and quatitative changes in relation to stated objectives

ex libris: from the books; precedes the owner's name on a bookplate, establishes ownership

exceptional child: child with a physical, mental, or learning abnormality who requires an admusted instructional program to meet his specific needs, as the slow learner, blind, and gifted

exogenous: originating outside the body; in disability analysis, a condition whose etiology is other than hereditary or genetic

exophoria: characteristic tendency for the eyes to turn outward when fusion is disrupted

exotropia: definitive outward turning of one eye; exophoria

expectancy level: learning expectancy level (L.E.L.); potential for learning based on intelligence and chronological age; can be compared to child's present performance in reading; various formulas can be utilized to determine L.E.L., as the following two well-known examples:

MA - 5 = L.E.L.*

Estimated reading level = no. years in school x $\frac{IQ}{100}$ +1**

expectancy table: any table with test scores along one axis and criterion categories along the other axis; entries showing number of individuals within score intervals who achieved at a given level on the

*Kaluger and Kolson
**Bond and Tinker

criterion variable, as 15 (out of 40) students were unable to recognize initial blends

expected grade placement: computed score based on the combining of mental and chronological age in which a particular level of achievement expressed in grade equivalent is specified

experience approach: development of basic reading skills through the use of written or dictated materials produced by learners about their experiences

experience background: the variety and depth of contact, direct or indirect, a person has had with various phenomena in the culture

experience chart: see chart, experience

experience method: see method, experience

experience-unit program: see program, experience-unit

experiential background: see background, experiential

expository material: see material, expository

expressive language skills: those abilities required to communicate ideas through language, such as writing and speaking

extrapolation: the process of estimating values of a function beyond the range of available data; extension of the curve beyond plotted points

extraversion: turning outward; an attitude characterized by an interest in things outside oneself in the physical and social environment

extreme scores: scores above or below the functional range limit (ceiling or floor) of a test

extrinsic: outside or external, as a reward of candy for achievement rather than self-satisfaction

extrinsic method: see method, extrinsic

extrinsic motivation: external reward, as candy or tokens

extrovert: person who is more interested in the physical and social environment than himself

eye dialect: transposing the spelling patterns of the school to a specific dialect of the population on words spoken in both, as does for duz

eye fixation: see fixation

eye-hand coordination: see coordination, eye-hand

eye movement record: see record, eye movement

eye movements: series of alternating pauses and quick movements of the eye which are the result of a change in the amount of stimulation delivered to the various external ocular muscles

eye movements, compensatory: adjustments for movements while reading

eye movements, pursuit: slow movements of the eyes when fixating on a moving object

eye movements, saccadic: quick, jerky movements characteristic of shifting fixation

eye physician: oculist, ophthalmologist

eye, preferred: eye an individual automatically prefers when viewing monocularly is required

eyedness: preference for use of one eye in perceptual-motor acts

eye-span: number of words or digits perceived in one fixation

eye-voice span: see span, eye-voice

Ff

face validity: see validity, face

facet: one of the several aspects of something, as reading is one facet of the language arts

factor: variable that seems to be partly responsible for the results of two or more tests, causing the correlation between or among tests; in general use, anything which is partially responsible for an outcome

factor analysis: statistical procedures employing intercorrelations among tests to identify the relative strength of the variables contributing to the test results, or to simply identify the common variables

factual material: objectively accurate presentation as opposed to a fanciful story

fairy tale: fanciful story as distinguished from reality or potential reality prose

families: groups of related elements; combinations of consonants and vowels which are sometimes taught together, as *en, at, in*

family, word: group of rhyming words which contain the same phonemic elements, as *bat, hat, fat*

fantasy: imaginative visualization momentarily controlled by the individual

far point: clear vision at a distance, measured by the Snellen test at twenty feet; other screening tests use a lens to normally focus at a comparable distant point

farsightedness: see hyperopia

feedback: sensory report resulting from behavior, as extent of movement or of pain; an evaluative reaction from a group after it has received some form of instruction

Fernald method: VAKT system in which the child learns to read and spell whole words; in stage 1 the word (written with crayon on a large strip of paper) is traced and pronounced in parts until the child can reproduce it without looking at the original; the child writes the word once on paper and once in an original sentence or story; the story is then typed to be read in print and the word is filed in a word bank; in stage 2 the procedure is the same but the tracing is eliminated; in stage 3 the child learns the word in print by saying it to himself and then writing it; finally in stage 4 new words are learned by recognizing their similarities to known words

Festschrift: memorial publication to honor a person, event, or anniversary

fiction: novel or tale composed from the imagination of the author; a branch of literature; a figment of one's imagination

figural: having the characteristics of a concrete object

figure ground perception: ability to select an object or form from the total field of incoming stimuli; the figure is the center of attention; the ground is the balance of the mass of stimuli

film library: organized collection of films, usually for a specific use in instruction; includes filmstrips, motion picture films, slides, film prints, etc.

filmstrip: short piece of film, about 30-50 inches long, which is projected on a screen from a special filmstrip projector for instructional purposes

final pitch contour: upward, downward, or level movement of the pitch of the voice at the end of an utterance, as *He is here.* (↑) *He is here?* (↑) *He is here . . .* (→)

fine motor activities: output through which the muscle system underlying delicate movements is exercised

finger agnosia: numbness of the fingers so that they do not respond to stimuli

finis: the end

finite system: system which has a limited number of units

fissure: cleavage or narrow grooves on the surface of the brain

fixation: suspension of psychological maturation; holding a visual focus on a part of a line of print in reading, as the eyes focus, sweep, focus, sweep, etc. across the line

fixation, frequency: incidence of fixations made per line of print

fixation pause: brief time in which the eye has stopped to focus in its uneven movement across a line of print

flaps: ends of a book jacket, which are folded in between the cover and the body of the book; author, biographical data, and/or a synopsis of the book are often found there

flash cards: individual cards with printed letters, words, numbers, or phrases used tachistoscopically by the teacher to introduce new material or to review sight words; can be rearranged in sequence or thought units

flashmeter: instrument for timed rapid exposure of items from a projector

flexibility, muscular: ability to move a limb through a range of positions using a joint as the fulcrum; flexibility is usually measured in degrees

flexibility, perceptual: ability to react in varied ways to stimuli

flexible binding: book binding at the spine allowing the book to open flat

flexible grouping: practice of re-grouping students temporarily for learning a specific skill

fluency in encoding: ability to effectively express oneself verbally

fly leaf: blank leaf at the beginning or end of a book

focal length: characteristic distance at which a lens yields clear, focused images of an object

font: complete type assortment of a specific size

foot-candle: unit of illumination thrown on a surface at right angles to the rays of a standard candle at one foot distant

footedness: preference for the right foot, or the left, for kicking, tapping, etc.

foreward: author's introduction of the reader to the contents, purpose, or organization of the book; may be written by an editor or some other person

form class: set of words that readily form similar phonetic or grammatical combinations with affixes, as the adjectives that form comparative with *er* and superlative with *est,* nouns that form plurals by adding *s*

form perception: ability to recognize the pattern of the elements making up the sequence of a whole, as *c-a-t* in *cat*

formal English: form of language which is used in classic literature, official

documents, and formal writing, in contrast to vernacular or colloquial (q.v.) form

format: general appearance and physical composition of a book

formative: derivational affix, one which determines the part of speech of
the derived word, as the *ness* in *harshness*

forms, alternate: see forms, equivalent

forms, equivalent: two tests that are parallel in content and difficulty and
are comparable in scores, variability, and reliability; usually standardized on the same population and published at the same time;
sometimes called alternate or duplicate forms

formula, Kuder-Richardson: estimate of the reliability of a test, based on
the mean, standard deviation, and number of items

$$r_{tt} = \left(\frac{n}{n-1}\right)\frac{\sigma^2 t - n\bar{p}\bar{q}}{\sigma^2 t}$$

where n = number of items in the test

σ_t = standard deviation of the test scores

$$\bar{p} = \frac{M_t}{n}$$

$$\bar{q} = 1 - \bar{p}$$

to the extent the items vary in difficulty this formula underestimates
the reliability; other methods of determining reliability of a test are:
(1) test-retest (2) alternate-forms (3) split-halves (Spearman-Brown
formula) q.v.

formula, readability: method of estimating the reading level of difficulty of
printed material by analyzing samples taken from the selection or
book; most popular formulas in use currently are (1) the Spache
Readability Formula, Primary (2) The Dale-Chall Readability
Formula (3) The Fry Readability Chart (4) The Lorge-Thorndike
Readability Formula (5) The Flesch Readability Formula and
(6) various experimental formulas using the "cloze" technique (q.v.);
most common factors in the formulas are: (1) number of hard words
(those not on a specific "easy word" list) (2) average sentence length
(3) average word length (number of syllables)

formula, Spearman-Brown: estimate of the reliability of a test by comparing the reliability of its split-halves (usually odd-numbered items vs. even-numbered items)

$$\text{Reliability of whole test} = \frac{2(\text{reliability of half-test})}{1 + (\text{reliability of half-test})}$$

see formula, Kuder-Richardson for further information on test reliability

fovea: depression in the center of the retina where the layers above the cones are thinner and the image falling there yields the clearest vision

fragment: part of a sentence

framing words: designating a word or group of words by placing the hands at each end simultaneously

free form: morpheme which has a distinct meaning of its own when used alone, as *dog*, but not the *s* in *dogs*

free reading: see reading, free

free vowel: vowel that may appear in an open syllable—one that does not end in a consonant, as *see, do*; but not *seed* or *dot*

frequency: in score tabulation, the number of persons getting the same score or falling within a group interval; in physics, the number of vibrations or waves occurring per second

frequency distribution: tabulation of test scores or tallies according to number of occurrences (frequencies) at each point on a scale

frequency polygon: graph showing the distribution of the frequencies for a given set of data

frequency, regression: number of back-sweeps (regression) of the eyes during the reading of a line of print

fricative: consonant voiced by forcing the breath through a narrow opening, as $/f/$ in *fact*

frontal: anterior part of an organ or the body; the forehead

fronted: sound produced farther forward by the tongue than the usual position

frontispiece: leaf containing an illustrative picture facing the title page of a book

frustrated: unsuccessful feelings associated with lack of goal accomplishment

frustration: affective state of one who cannot satisfy a need or meet a goal

51

frustration level: maximum performance level beyond which the individual cannot perform without excessive error

frustration reading level: see reading level, frustration

function words: words that signal a relationship, such as chronology or cause-effect

functional: valuable for adjustment or orientation

functional literacy: level of reading ability which is necessary to function in our society; somewhere around fourth- to seventh-grade level

functional range: range of new scores within which one can interpret individual scores safely in terms of the standard error of measurement

fundamental processes: basic skills

fundus: base of a body organ; in vision, the back of the eye

fused: refers to subjects that are closely related being taught as one subject, as the language arts which include reading, speaking, writing, and spelling

fusion: visually, the process of bringing together into one perception the images that are seen by the two eyes

Gg

g: symbol for general factor of intelligence as described by British psychologist Spearman

games: specially developed materials designed to act as learning and reinforcement tools for a variety of skill areas

gazette: newspaper

gazetteer: dictionary of geographical terms

gender identity: expression of persistent behavior representing one's maleness or femaleness or ambivalence in same

gender role: public expression by words and behavior reflecting gender identity (q.v.)

gene: submicroscopic structure in chromosomes; physical unit of heredity

general vocabulary: words used in daily listening, speaking, reading, and writing

generalization: principle with general application; the process of drawing a conclusion or concept from a number of specific facts or observations

generalized movement: movement that is reflected in the whole body in contrast to a specific concentrated movement of a single member of the body such as the right hand

generative grammar: language model that shows how all the grammar is developed from a sequence of applied rules

generative-transformational grammar: grammar assigning structural descriptions to sentences and relating their deep structures and meanings to their surface structures and sounds

generic: broadly applicable to all members of a class as contrasted to specific

genotype: genetic composition of an individual determined by genes and chromosomes, reflected only through interaction with its environment; the observable product is the phenotype

Gerstman syndrome: group of symptoms showing a lack of laterality and a distubrance of body image, as agraphia, left-right disorientation, and finger agnosia; a disorder of cerebral functioning

gerund: verb used as a noun and ending in -*ing,* as in the word *fighting,* in *fighting is forbidden*

gestalt: unified whole which is not identifiable as the sum of its parts, a psychological theory

gifted: those who demonstrate a high level of learning ability with IQ of two standard deviations above the mean or higher; talented

Gillingham method: highly structured VAKT system that proposes five lessons a week for a minimum of two years—at first the child learns individual letter sounds and is then taught to blend them into words; tracing is utilized in teaching both symbol and sound; spelling is taught simultaneously

gland: organ or cell which discharges a secretion used elsewhere in the body to enhance its function, as the *thyroid gland*

global: perceiving something in its entirety without an attempt to distinguish separate parts or functions, as a global response is a generalized response rather than specific

glossary: alphabetical arrangement of difficult or specialized terms with explanations or definitions; usually found in the back of a book

gnosia: perceiving and understanding

goals: aims, overall purposes

grade chronological age (GCA): age corresponding to a given actual school grade in years and months

grade equivalent: see score, grade placement

grade expectancy: relationship between chronological age and grade; the chronological age minus 5 gives the grade placement, e.g., age 11 yrs., 6 mos. minus 5 gives a grade placement of 6th grade, 6th month

grade norm: average test score of pupils at a given grade level

grade placement: indicates months in grade; one month is assigned for each of the ten school months, so 6.2 is sixth grade, second month, or October of the sixth year

grade placement equivalent: score assigned to pupils in a given grade on the basis of chronological age, mental age, or other characteristics

grade score: average achievement level in terms of grade and month

graded reader: see reader, graded

gradient: rate of modification in relative strength or weakness of a response

grammar: study of the system and structure of language; possible arrangement of words in a language

grammar, case: combination of the syntactic-semantic relationship features as theorized by Fillmore

grammatic closure: auditory vocal habits of syntax and grammar learned automatically and used to predict future choices

grammatical: conforming to the rules of grammar

grammatical marking: inflecting of words according to form class, as the class, nouns, because they can be marked for "plural": *boy, boys; house, houses*

grapheme: written or printed counterpart of a phoneme; a written language symbol that represents oral language

graphology: the study of handwritten forms of a language

gridiron effect: arrangement of letters in a word so they all have the same slant, as *bottle*

grip age: see age, grip

gross agility: ability to coordinate body movements quickly and accurately, as in the activity of getting up and down speedily

gross motor activity: movement in which groups of large muscles are employed and rhythm and balance are of major importance

group test: see test, group

group therapy: see therapy, group

grouping: placing children by achievement level, special learning needs, or interests to promote more effective learning

grouping, ability: placing children with the same characteristics together for instruction; homogeneous grouping

grouping, heterogeneous: placing children together for instruction without regard to ability, achievement, or other learning characteristics

grouping, homogeneous: see grouping, ability

grouping, need: grouping plan in which the child is placed on the basis of a specific instructional weakness in a skill area

grouping, tracking or stream: organizational plan in which children are placed at slow, average, and fast levels for instruction and remain at those levels for a length of time (one year or more)

guide words: boldface words at the top of a dictionary page used in quickly selecting the page on which a word may be found

guidebook: handbook for travelers with information about a city, region, or country; handbook concerning a building, museum, etc.; a manual

guided reading: reading lesson in which the teacher identifies a purpose for reading the basal reader selection; the children read silently, discuss the selection orally, then an individual may reread a part of the selection orally for specific purposes

guiding question: question used by the teacher to form the basis for reading through a selection

gyrus: fold on the surface of the cortex of the brain

gyrus, angular: area of the left hemisphere of the brain which controls speech functions; when abnormal, may cause learning difficulties in right-handed individuals

Hh

hallucination: false sensory perception of an external object or person when nothing is present; may occur in any of the five senses

halo effect: tendency to rate an individual consistently high or low on the basis of subjective general impression

handbook: small book serving as reference or guidance, as a teacher's manual

handedness: perferential choice of one hand to lead in various activities

handicapped, hearing: defective hearing, ranging from hard-of-hearing to the deaf

haptic perception: process of getting information through two modalities: kinesthesis and touch

Harris Jacobson Core *Basic Elementary Reading Vocabularies:* frequency word count list gleaned from reading materials K-6, arranged by levels (general) and technical subject areas

Hawthorne effect: condition arising in an experimental study which alters subjects' performance due to their awareness and interest as participants in the research

HC: available in hard copy form, as indicated in ERIC publications such as RIE (q.v.)

head movement: extraneous head movements during reading

hearing aid: compact amplifier used in certain hearing loss cases to increase hearing efficiency by increasing sound intensity

hearing loss, conduction: loss of hearing acuity as a result of a reduction or total elimination of sound transmission to the inner ear, where receptors are located in the cochlea

hearing loss, sensory-neural: loss of acuity as a result of a defect or disease of the cochlea or acoustic nerve

hearing vocabulary: words a person understands on an oral level; may or may not be able to speak, read, or write them

hebetude: emotional dullness or disinterest

Hegge-Kirk-Kirk: drill method of developing sound-symbol relationships, left-to-right progression and gestalt closure; associational devices and the grapho-vocal method are utilized to teach letter sounds; drills are used for overlearning, and the individual sounds are blended into words

height age: see age, height

hemiatrophy: atrophy limited to one side of an organ or part of the body

hemiopia: blindness in one half of visual field for one or both eyes

hemiplegia: paralysis of a single side of the body

hemispheres: left and right halves into which the cerebrum is divided

hemispheric dominance: see dominance, cerebral

hemoglobin: protein pigment of the red blood corpuscles which carries oxygen to the tissues and returns with carbon dioxide to the lungs

heterogeneous: composed of parts which represent a wide range of difference or variability; antonym to homogeneous

heterogeneous grouping: see grouping, heterogeneous

heteronym: word having a different sound and meaning from another but with the same spelling, as *row* in *row the boat* and *row* in *they got into a row*

heterophoria: lack of balance between the muscles of the eyes, so that one eye deviates abnormally when fusion is broken

heuristic: self-discovery learning as opposed to directed instruction

hieroglyphics: ancient writing system, especially Egyptian, in which pictures stood for a word, sound, or idea

histogram: graphic representation of a frequency distribution consisting of series of contiguous rectangles in which the height of each rectangle represents the frequency for each score

histrionic: acting in an artificial or affected manner

holdings: volumes and other materials comprising the acquisitions of a library

home visitation: an agency's staff member visit to a home with the intent of gathering information through interview and/or observation; to be utilized in arriving at specific recommendations for resolution of a referred problem

homeostasis: maintenance of equilibrium in the bodily processes

homogeneous: composed of similar parts which represent a narrow range of variability

homogeneous grouping: see grouping, ability

homograph: word which has two or more different derivations and meanings, as *bark* of a tree and hear the dog *bark*

homolateral: on the same side of the body

homologous: body structures with essentially the same origin, as the *arm* of a man and the *fin* of a *fish*

homonym: word having the same sound as another but different in meaning, origin, and generally spelling, as *meat, meet,* and *mete*

homophone: words that are pronounced the same but spelled differently, as *be* and *bee*

hormone: chemical substance produced by one organ and transmitted to other organs via the lymph or blood; this substance has very specific effects on the receiving organ

hornbook: primer or book of rudiments initially containing the alphabet and religious tract used for teaching reading during the American colonial period; the paper was covered with a sheet of transparent horn, framed and a handle attached

hostility: form of behavior in which there is a tendency to feel anger toward and desire harm to a person or group

hour, library: scheduled time an individual, group, or classes spend in the library

house organ: periodical issued by a company or organization dealing with the activities of its members or the company

humor, aqueous: fluid filling the anterior chamber of the eye between the cornea and the lens

humor, vitreous: transparent semifluid situated between the retina and the lens of the eye

hydrocephalus: condition characterized by excessive amount of cerebro-spinal fluid within the skull, which produces enlargement of the head and atrophy of the brain

hygiene, mental: science and process of maintaining wholesome person-ality, good adjustment to life, and positive relationships

hyperactivity: excessive activity or energy

hyperacusis: extremely efficient auditory acuity

hyperkinesis: overactivity or excessive motor movement

hypermetabolism: metabolism above normal limits

hypermetropia: *syn.,* hyperopia

hyperope: a person who has hyperopia; a farsighted individual

hyperopia: condition in which light rays focus behind the retina instead of on it; farsightedness

hyperopic astigmatism: see astigmatism, hyperopic

hyperphoria: type of heterophoria which involves upward deviation of the line of sight during fusion disruption

hyperthymia: overactivity of the individual; exaggerated emotional response

hyperthyroidism: condition caused by excessive thyroid activity and characterized by increased basal metabolism

hypertropia: see hyperphoria

hypoactivity: pronounced lack of physical activity

hypochondriasis: persistent preoccupation with one's physical or emo-tional health; accompanied by bodily complaints without apparent pathology

hypacusia, hypoacusia: impairment of auditory acuity due to loss of sensitivity either conductive or sensory-neural

hypokinesis: lack of normal bodily movement and motor activity

hypometabolism: metabolic rate below normal limits

hypophoria: type of heterophoria which involves downward deviation of the line of sight during the moment of disrupted fusion

hypopituitarism: deficient secretion of the pituitary gland characterized by short stature, defective growth and sex activity, and mental torpor

hypothesis: tentative theory or assumption

hypothyroidism: condition caused by limited thyroid activity and characterized by lowered basal metabolism

hypotropia: see hypophoria

hypoxia: low oxygen content in the inhaled air

hysteria: condition resulting from emotional conflicts manifested by dramatic physical symptoms; characterized by immaturity, dependency, and the use of the defense mechanisms of conversion and dissociation

Ii

idealization: unconscious overestimation of an admired characteristic of another; put "on a pedestal"

identification: unconscious act of emotionally associating oneself closely with another person or group

idioglossia: distortion of regular language due to omission, substitution, and transposition of speech sounds; *syn.,* idiolalia

idiograph: symbol that represents or is associated with a person, a thing, or a concept, as a *skull and crossbones* on a medicine bottle represents *poison*

idiolect: individual's personal version of the standard language

idiom: form of expression which, understood in its entirety, has a different meaning from the literal meaning of its parts, as *Shake a leg!*

idiopathic: coined by an individual, or of unknown origin

idiot: individual who is feebleminded and in adulthood has an IQ not above 25 as measured on an individual intelligence test such as the Stanford Binet or Wechsler

illumination, level of: measurement in foot-candles of the light falling on a surface

illusion: misinterpretation of real, external experience

illustrator, book: artist who does the pictorial illustrations of a book

image: revived mental sense experience, in the absence of the sensory stimulus

image, retinal: replica of the object, formed on the retina of the eye

imagery: mental pictures, or the imagining of things or events

imbalance, lateral: tendency of the muscles of the eyes to pull the eye inward or outward from normal position, as in *esophoria* or *exophoria*

imbalance, muscular: lack of muscular balance between eye muscles, causing heterophoria or strabismus

imbalance, vertical: incorrect functioning of the muscles of the eye(s), pulling upward or downward, as in *hyperphoria* or *hypophoria*

imbecile: individual who is feebleminded with adult IQ between 25 and 50 as measured on an individual intelligence test, such as the Stanford Binet or Wechsler; between classification of idiot and educable

immaturity: not fully developed, youthful; opposite of maturity

immediate constituents: two parts of a construction, as *do* an *catche* in *dogcatcher*

imperception: cognitive inability to interpret sensory information correctly

impletion: process of filling or state of being filled

implied meaning: see comprehension, inferential

imprint: name of the owner or the publisher tamped on the binding or at the bottom of the title paper

impulse: a psychic striving; a sudden and spontaneous action made without reflection

impulsiveness: tendency to act hastily without thinking through the consequences of the act

incentive: motive for acting a certain way; may strengthen the drive toward an objective by adding value to it

incidental teaching: instruction introduced because it is timely, adding learning by-products to those of the planned immediate goal(s)

increment: amount or rate of progressive change

independent activities: tasks performed by a learner when not directly involved in a teacher-directed group

independent reading: easy reading material on which the child can proceed without help, with the ratio of unknown words not more than one in two hundred running words and a comprehension level of 90%

index: alphabetical list of names and topics to be found in a book with their page references, usually at the back of the book

index, periodical: cumulative alphabetical ist of topics to be found in a periodical(s), issued annually or at some other time interval

individual differences: see differences, individual

individual test: see test, individual

individualization: adaptation of instruction to the learning needs of a specific pupil

individualized reading: see reading, individualized

induction: process of developing generalizations from specific cases by reasoning; moving from part-to-whole, as in the synthetic phonics method

inductive reasoning: form of thinking that moves from the particular to the general

infantile myxedema: advanced deficiency of thyroid hormone starting in infancy due to injury or disease of the thyroid gland

infantilism: childish behavior persisting into adulthood

inference: logical conclusion from given data

inflected form: word to which an inflectional ending (q.v.) has been added, as *reads,* where *s* is added to the root word, *read*

inflection: rise and fall of voice pitch in speech

inflectional ending: suffix which has meaning and indicates number, tense, possessive, comparison, present participle, or third person singular, as hill*s*, Bill'*s*, long*er*, play*ing*, sing*s*

informal reading: independent reading for pleasure or information, initiated by the individual

Informal Reading Inventory (IRI): test in which the individual reads through a graded series of selections, easy to difficult, until he reaches his frustration level; the teacher records all errors in pronunciation, vocabulary, and comprehension; from the results the teacher determines independent, instructional, and frustration levels; usually the selections are excerpts from basal readers

informal test: see test, informal

information theory: interdisciplinary study, of which communications theory is the technology, dealing with the transmission of signals or the communication of information; it draws upon cybernetics, engineering, linguistics, physics, psychology, and sociology

inhibiting factors: those forces or conditions that interfere with normal learning

inhibition: mental or physical condition wherein a function or a circumstance prevents the expression of some other function

initial consonant: see consonant, initial

Initial Teaching Alphabet (i.t.a.): see alphabet, Augmented Roman

innate response system: unlearned motor responses present at birth

inner language: process in which experiences are internalized and organized without the use of language symbols

inner speech: "hearing" the words as they are read silently; subvocal movements of the voice mechanism

innervation: actual excitation of a muscle or gland through an efferent nerve

input, output: the process of receiving stimulus (input), the action resulting from processing of the stimulus; i.e., verbal, motor, etc. (output)

insert: page added to a bound book, printed separately from the regular book pages

insertions: letters, syllables, or words added by the reader in oral reading

insight: full understanding of the meaning and relevance of a situation or act

instruction, differentiated: multiple classroom learning situations which approach the ideal of meeting each individual's needs

instruction, individual: type of learning situation in which each child works at his own materials geared to his needs and periodically interacts with the teacher

instruction, library: teaching learners to use the library effectively

instructional aide: teacher's helper in the classroom

instructional level: highest reading level at which effective teaching can be initiated

intact modality: modality found to be superior in someone with deficits; instruction is geared to this modality, as the child who has a strong visual and weak auditory ability would be taught through a visual approach

integrated: subject taught as a unified whole though it may be drawn from several subject areas; as *social studies,* drawn from *geography, history, economics, government, and sociology*

integration: relating and organizing dispersed ideas or stimuli into a unified response

Intellectual Status Index (ISI): derived score developed by the California Test Bureau, similar to a ratio IQ, using the average chronological age of pupil with identical grade placement instead of the child's actual chronological age

intelligence: individual's ability to perceive relationships such as logical, spatial, numerical, and verbal, to learn to recall, and to solve problems; sometimes referred to as mental age or scholastic aptitude; measured by verbal and nonverbal performance tests

intelligence, nonverbal: level of performance in using abstract signs and symbols

intelligence quotient (IQ): ratio of mental age (MA), as determined by a test of mental abilities, to chronological age (CA) for an individual

$$IQ = \frac{MA}{CA} \times 100$$

intelligence quotient (IQ), deviation: index of brightness expressed by the performance of individuals of comparable chronological age; standard score scale represented by M = 100, $\sigma = 16$

intelligence quotient (IQ), ratio: see intelligence quotient

intelligence test: see test, intelligence

intelligence, verbal: level of performance in dealing with language

intensity: a sound's measured physical size; the strength of any sensory data or behavior

intensive reading: see reading, intensive

interage groups: placement of children with differing age or grade levels within one classroom for instructional purposes

interest: feeling of desire for, being attracted to, or a concern about something

interest inventory: listing which reflects the individual's preferences for reading, working, or playing; often used by teachers as a guide for initiating instruction as an aid in book selection

interfixation: eye movements from fixation-to-fixation during reading

interlibrary loan: loan transacted between libraries for the library use or for an individual

internal consistency: estimate of the comparability of two parts of a test given at one time

interneurosensory learning: learning that takes place due to the related functioning of two or more systems in combination, as *auditory-visual, tactile-kinesthetic*

interoceptor: sense organ receptor within the body, as opposed to the exteroceptor at the body surface

interpolation: process of estimating a point which falls between two known points on a curve; often used to establish a norm table for translating test scores into all grade level scores

interpretive comprehension: see comprehension, inferential

intersensory integration: see cross-modal perception

interval, class: unit of a grouped frequency distribution wherein the range of scores within that unit is assumed to be at midpoint for statistical computation or graphic interpretation

intonation: rise and fall of voice pitch during speech

intonation contour or pattern: sequence of rising and falling pitches through the sentence

intonation system: linguistic system which deals with a specific spoken language's pitch, stress, and juncture (q.v.)

intraneurosensory learning: learning primarily occuring through one sense modality

intrauterine: located or taking place within the uterus

intrinsic motivation: desire within oneself to achieve well, simply for the satisfaction derived therefrom

introjection: unconcious mental mechanism in which loved or hated objects are taken within oneself symbolically; opposite of projection

introversion: type of personality trait in which interests, thoughts, and feelings are directed inward toward oneself

inventory: profiling of an individual's attitudes, behavior, or interests, which is gathered for a purpose; it has no right or wrong answers; it typifies the responses of the individual

inventory, adjustment (personality): standard performance instrument through which the individual reflects his personal and social adjustment, temperament, and/or mental health

inventory, study-skills: list of the study skills of students differentiating those learned from those not learned

inversion: change in the usual declarative word order, as *He is coming* (*Is he coming?*)

ipsilateral: occuring on the same side; homolateral, as the individual who is *right-handed* and *right-eyed*

IRI: abbreviation for Informal Reading Inventory (q.v.)

iris: muscular pigmented diaphram, with an aperture in its center, which controls the light rays falling on the retina; it accommodates the eye to the intensity of the light rays

irregular: not conforming to the general rule; *women* is an irregular noun plural (not *womans*) and *sang* is an irregular past tense (*not singed*)

irrelevant material: facts or information unrelated to the topic being discussed

i.t.a.: abbreviation for Initial Teaching Alphabet (q.v.)

item: individual question or problem on a test

item analysis: process of examining a test item to determine its difficulty and its discrimination value

item structure: evidence of relationship: between items, between items and scores, between items and criteria, and the function of distractors; determined by the statistical procedure of item analysis

itinerant teacher: teacher who moves from school to school and teaches individuals or small groups of children who leave their regular classroom for the scheduled special sessions

Jj

Joplin plan: organizational interclass grouping in which children who are reading on approximately the same grade level are brought together for reading instruction regardless of their regular grade placement; following the reading period, the children return to their regular classroom; the plan was popularized in Joplin, Missouri

journal: periodical published by an institution or learned society with articles covering topics within the specialty of the association; a regular record of the activities of a person or a public body

jumping: the ability to leap up in the air or over simple objects without falling

juncture: a pause in the flow of oral language that indicates meaning, as between the two words *an addition,* before and after a word in apposition (*my son, Jack,*) and between words of cardinal counting (*one, two, three*); sometimes, but not always, represented by the punctuation *comma, colon,* or *semicolon*

juvenile books: see books, juvenile

Kk

kernel sentence: an earlier term of generative-transformational grammar describing active, positive, and declarative sentences from which passive, negative, imperative, and interrogative sentences could be formed

key, scoring: sheet which contains the correct responses to be used in scoring a test

key word: see word, key

kinesthesis: sensory impression of movement or strain in muscles, tendons, or joints

kinesthetic: see kinesthesis; learning through the use of body movement sensations

kinesthetic imagery: muscle imagery or a revived sense of body movement, not actual movement

kinesthetic method: see method, kinesthetic

kinesthetic perception: see perception, kinesthetic

kinetic: pertaining to motion

kinetic overshoot: movements of the hand in writing that push the pen beyond the desired point

kinetic reversal: see reversal, kinetic

knowledge: learning that contributes to the individual's intellectual functioning

Kuder-Richardson formula: formula for estimating content reliability of a test through an analysis of internal consistency; see formula, Kuder-Richardson

Ll

labial: sound articulated mainly by the lips, as /*wh*/, /*w*/, /*f*/, /*v*/, /*b*/, /*p*/, and /*m*/

labialization: formation of sounds with the lips without audible utterance, as /*w*/ in *way*

lacuna: a gap or missing part, as in memory or a library collection

lalopathy: any speech disorder

language: an established system of oral communication; spoken or written symbols representing conventional meanings

language arts: an area of the school curriculum which deals with communication skills—reading, writing, speaking, listening, and spelling

language experience method: method of teaching reading which includes both the receptive and expressive aspects of language, using story content dictated or developed from the children's personal experience or ideas; instructional stages include oral discussion, story dictation, story reading, word recognition and/or word attack activities, development of word banks, and recreational reading

language, inner: organizing and internalizing experiences without the use of language symbols

language pathology: study of the etiology and treatment of disorders of symbolic behavior

language rhythm clue: see clue, language rhythm

language therapy: see therapy, language

language-type experience records: class, group, or individually dictated statements which are "read" by the children to develop and reinforce language facility

71

larynx: organ at the top of the trachea containing the vocal cords, essential to the production of voice; the voice box

lateral confusion: see mixed laterality

lateral dominance: see dominance, lateral

lateral imbalance: see imbalance, lateral

lateral muscular imbalance: see muscular imbalance, lateral

lateral phoria: see phoria, lateral

laterality: the awareness of the two sides of one's body, the ability to identify them as left or right correctly, and the ability to perform different motor activities in which a dominant side is most efficient

Latinate grammar: grammatical description of language using principles and terminology derived from descriptions of Latin

law of directional constancy: recognition that a shape or form is dependent upon the stability of its positional rotation, e.g., *b* and *d*

law of form constancy: recognition of a form is dependent upon the absence of modifications, *Q* and *O*

law of object constancy: perception of a given form occurs despite positional and morphologic alterations, as a chair is seen as a chair despite differences in the stimulus pattern on the retina as the viewer changes relative position

lax: pronounced with very little muscular tension in the articulators: as /z/ is lax, whereas /s/ is tense

lead (lēd): short summary serving as the introduction to a news article

lead (lĕd): in printing, a metal strip placed between lines of print to add space

learner: the student or pupil who is being instructed and is learning (q.v.)

learning: undergoing changes in behavior and/or performance due to experience

learning and reading disability, primary: generally an individual of normal mental ability whose learning deficit is associative rather than perceptual

learning, associative: items experienced together tend to be connected so that one evokes the other; the ability of the learner to relate meanings to words or other symbols

learning disability: retardation or delayed development in one or more of the processes of speech, language, or reading which is not due to mental retardation, cultural, or instructional factors, but from a psychological handicap, possibly of cerebral origin, and/or behavioral or emotional disturbance

learning disability specialist: individual who, as a member of a child study team, has the responsibility of examining and classifying children considered handicapped and recommending special programs for them; sometimes a specialist also does remedial work directly with children

learning evaluation: assessment after instruction to determine the degree of mastery attained in the skill taught

learning experiences: instructional program situations devised to meet the obligatives set forth in the educational curriculum

learning machine: term sometimes applied to a mechanical teaching machine which is programmed for self-instruction

learning, rote: memorization by frequent repetition with little or no attention devoted to meaning

Leavell Hand-Eye Coordinator: a slanted drawing board instrument with mounted stereoscopic lenses and a clip for slides which are traced

left-right direction: arbitrary direction in which English is read or written

left-to-right progression: skill of inspecting words or reading lines of print from left to right

legasthemia: inability to make correct associations with printed symbols

legibility: quality of type, spacing, and format of written or printed material which makes it readable with ease

leisure reading: see reading, recreational

L.E.L.: stands for learning expectancy level, which may be derived by subtracting 5 from the mental age

lens: see crystalline lens

lesions: any alteration in tissue, such as a wound or a scar, due to injury or disease

lesson plan: brief statement of the objectives, materials needed, and sequence of procedures to be used in an instructional period; serves as a guide

letter, ascending: letter of print, or writing, that extends above the shoulder of the type body, as *b, d, h,* etc.

letter, descending: letter which extends below the line of printing, as *p, q, g*

letter phonics: see phonics, letter

letter phonogram: see phonogram, letter

letter-sound correspondence: see sound-symbol connection

level: related group or components designed to develop a specific cluster of skills, connoting a hierarchy; position on a scale or ordered series

level of illumination: see illumination, level of

level, reading capacity: highest level at which a person can comprehend what is read to him orally

levography: mirror writing

lexical: referring to the words of a language; or, all the linguistic signs or morphemes of a language

lexicographer: compiler of a dictionary, specializing in derivation, usage, and meaning of words

lexicon: total set of morphemes and words in a language; a dictionary

lexigraphic: as found in a dictionary

librarian: individual who has been educated in the field of library science and is engaged in library service

library classification systems: include alphabetic-classed filing system, author card, book number, call number, decimal classification, Library of Congress classification, subject entry, title entry (q.v. each)

library, classroom: collection of books in the classroom, usually drawn from the school library, the public library, or a mobile library; books should, at any given time, meet the reading needs of the range of abilities of the pupils in the room

library, film: see film library

library hour: see hour, library

library instruction: see instruction, library

Library of Congress Classification: organizational system for library books which allows for expansion; uses letters and numbers:

A	General Works	G	Geography and Anthropology
B	Philosophy and Religion	H	Social Sciences
C	History	J	Political Science
D	Foreign History	K	Law
EF	American History	L	Education

M Music	S Agriculture
N Fine Arts	T Technology
P Language and Literature	U Militiary Science
Q Science	V Naval Science
R Medicine	Z Bibliography and Library Science

Librium (chlordiazepoxide): minor benzodiazepine tranquilizer used to treat hyperactive, aggressive children and reduce tension and anxiety in adults; may stimulate some children; dosage including adult range: 10-300 mg daily

limited edition: publication of a limited number of copies or a special quality edition, in addition to the regular one

line graph: a diagram showing the relationship between two variables, e.g., diagram showing performance over a period of time, with time shown on the abscissa (⟶) and level of performance on the ordinate (⭡), and the coordinate points connected by straight or curved lines

linguals: sounds formed by the tongue, as /l/ and /r/

linguist: scholar whose training is in the field of languages

linguistics: scientific study of the nature and function of language

lip movement: see movement, lip

lisping: defective articulation of the silibants /s/ and /z/ as *thing* for *sing*

listening comprehension: see comprehension, listening

listening vocabulary: see vocabulary, listening

literal comprehension: see comprehension, literal

lobes of the brain: sectional areas of the brain: frontal lobe at the forehead, occipital lobe at the lower rear, temporal at the lower side, and parietal at the upper rear

local norms: normative results from testings conducted in a local school system; used for comparative study instead of national norms furnished by the test makers

location clue: in reading, a suggestion as to the placement of a passage or answer in the sequence of the story or article; generally, a suggestion as to the geographical or spatial placement

location skills: ability to quickly and accurately find a specific segment of information, as entries in a reference work or a specific date

locomotion: motor behavior in moving from one place to another, as crawling, walking, hopping, etc.

locomotor agility: skipping, hopping, and other locomotor behavior done with relative ease and speed

logograph: symbol representing a unit of meaning rather than a unit of sound; morpheme instead of phoneme, as ¢, Σ

logopedics (lŏ-gō-pē-dics): diagnosis and correction of speech and voice disabilities

"long" vowel: vowel that says its own name, as /a/ in *make,* /e/ in *mete,* /o/ in *hope*

look-say method: whole word learning method by seeing it and saying it; sight method of instruction

loudness: psychological aspect of sound primarily dependent upon individual response to intensity of tone, fundamental frequency, and overtone structure

lower case: small form of a letter, as distinguished from capital letter form

low-level phonological rule: rule covering some unimportant characteristic of a phoneme pronunciation, as a nasal consonant must be voiced

Mm

McDade Method: see method, non-oral

McGinnis CID or Association Method: system in which the child is taught the articulation of isolated speech sounds and then a sequence of several sounds; this is followed by writing and reading the sequences before picture-word association, as saying sounds *c-ar-t,* then reading and writing *c-ar-t,* and finally associating this sequence with a picture of a cart; the words are then learned by memory and sentences are introduced first by rote; kinesthetic reinforcement and color coding of the vowels and consonants are used; this method is utilized for treating aphasia, both receptive and expressive

McGuffey Readers: the first articulated basal reading series used in American schools

machine-scoring: process of scoring a test with the aid of a mechanical or electrical device which counts and records the responses made using mark-sensing, punched hole, or electronic scanning techniques

macron: straight line placed horizontally over a vowel to indicate that it has the long sound, as, *dōme*; a diacritical mark

macula, lutea: a yellowish, oval depression at the center of the retina of the eye where the clearest vision occurs

Maddox rod: glass rod used with a small light source to test for aphoria (q.v.)

magazine: periodical for public's reading, containing articles by a number of authors, usually characterized by general topical articles and special continuing sections

main card: see card, main

main entry: see entry, main

main heading: title or short statement of the main topic in a chapter or other composition

main idea: chief idea of a sentence, paragraph, or selection

mainstreaming: placing of handicapped children in the regular classroom for the major portion of their educational program

major premise: in a syllogism, the proposition containing the general truth from which the particular inference is deduced

maladjustment: position in which a person falls short of being able to do what is expected of him

management, classroom: teacher behaviors that determine and control the type of learning setting in the classroom day-to-day

mandible: the upper or lower jaw

mania: mental illness characterized by acceleration of speech, thought, and bodily movements, excitability and mood elation

manic-depressive psychosis: major mental illness marked by severe mood swings, from highs to lows and vice versa

manual expression: motor encoding; expression of ideas through gestures

manuscript: author's original work presented to an editor or printer for publication; the handwritten or cursive form as distinguished from the printed form

manuscript writing: see writing, manuscript

mapping: a pattern of symbols that corresponds exactly with a physical feature, geography, or a system of events such as brain waves

marginal vocabulary: potential vocabulary

mark-sensing: pertaining to a system of machine-scoring tests using an electrical contact to "sense" responses made with a special pencil

masking: partial or total interference with perception of an auditory stimulus by presenting a second auditory stimulus at the same time

mastery: performance on a test which meets or betters the criterion level

matched groups: two groups, equated on specific variables such as intelligence, age, sex, etc; an experimental and a control group

material, expository: written material that sets forth facts and ideas

material, narrative: reading matter that tells a story

materials, audio-visual: visual and auditory teaching aids, such as films, film strips, records, tapes, slides, etc.

maturation: physiological, mental, and neurological development consistent with chronological age

maturational lag: delay in physiological, mental, or neurological development of areas without obvious structural defect

maturity: state of being fully developed in form and function

maturity, emotional: control of affective behavior consistent with the age or stage of development

maturity, mental: level of intellectual development at a given age; intellectual capacity

maximum-performance test: test which measures optimum performance, as an intelligence or achievement test, as opposed to a typical-performance test (personality)

mean, arithmetic: sum of a set of scores divided by the number of scores; arithmetic average; a measure of central tendency

mean deviation (MD): average deviation from the mean

meaning, sentence: idea conveyed by the total sentence as opposed to the ideas conveyed through phrases or clauses

meaning unit: see unit, meaning

meaning, vocabulary: see vocabulary, meaning

measurement: assessment of a characteristic (e.g., reading ability, height, personality) using an objective or subjective device, and comparison of results with some standard amount of that characteristic; provides the basis for making qualitative judgments

meatus (mē-ā-tus): passageway from the outer ear to the eardrum membrane

mechanics of reading: habits developed in relation to reading but apart from the reading process itself, as following lines of print from left to right, and from one page to another

medial consonant: see consonant, medial

medial sound: see sound, medial

median: point on a distribution arranged in a ranked order which divides the distribution into two equal groups, 50% above and 50% below; the 50th percentile

medulla oblongata: bulblike structure at the top of the spinal cord, connecting it to the pons (q.v.)

melancholia: pathological dejection, usually psychotic

memory: ability to store and retrieve previously experienced sensations and perceptions, even when the stimulus is no longer present; imagery; recall, retention

memory, long-term (LTM): relatively permanent stored information which is capable of retrieval through association

memory, rote: reproduction of learned material without regard to meaning

memory, short-term (STM): limited capacity memory of short duration which dissipates with time or is replaced by new information

memory span: number of items one is capable of recalling immediately after their presentation has ended

mental ability: intelligence, mental maturity

mental age: see age, mental

mental age grade placement: grade level according to results of a test of mental ability

mental deficiency: see deficiency, mental

mental hygiene: see hygiene, mental

mental maturity: see maturity, mental

mental measurement: quantitative determination of a person's mental abilities

mental set: attitude

metabolism: chemical process whereby food is utilized by cells and organs of the body to produce protoplasm (anabolism) and in turn is broken down into simpler compounds (catabolism) exchanging energy

metabolism, basal: minimum energy expenditure necessary for the vital functions while the individual is at rest but not asleep

metacarpal: five elongated bones of the hand located between the wrist and fingers

metaphor: a figure of speech in which a word literally denoting one kind of object or idea is used in place of another in order to suggest an analogy between them, as *He is a work horse,* meaning *He works hard like a horse*

method, alphabet-spelling: instructional approach which teaches the names of the letters first, then the names of letters in a word in sequence, and then the pronunciation of the word; widely used from 17th through 19th century

method, analytical: reading method which initially presents the whole word, followed by a breakdown into smaller parts; this analysis of the words provides correct pronunciation, as in the Scott Foresman Readers

method, auto-instructional: procedures used to present lessons in short, sequential steps progressing from simple to complex levels in the development of a skill, with immediate knowledge of results and continuous involvement of the learner

method, case: see case study

method, experience: reading instruction method that uses children's actual experiences and records them in the children's own language for their reading exercises

method, extrinsic: learner's goals are extraneous rather than those inherent in the learning activity itself, as reading to earn a reward of candy or reading to please the teacher

method, kinesthetic: using muscle movement to supplement the auditory and visual stimuli in remediation, as tracing the word forms with the finger

method, look-and-say: see method, sight

method, McDade: see method, non-oral

method, Miles Peep Hole: method for observing eye movements employing a small opening near the middle of a page between two lines of print so the observer can watch pupil's eye movements through the hole

method, mirror: method whereby the examiner holds a mirror at a slight angle to the reading material to watch the eye movements of the readers

method, New Castle: whole-class reading instruction method, emphasizing phonics, which utilizes filmstrips parallel to, but not identical with, basal lesson

method, non-oral: silent reading instructional teaching method initiated in the 1940's by McDade of Chicago which attempted to develop a direct, meaningful response to printed words without accompanying speech; words were shown in combination with pictures, objects, and actions in a non-oral preparation period; oral symbol and printed symbol were never shown together

method, oral: reading instructional method using reading aloud for growth in skills and for evaluation of sight vocabulary and the other word attack skills

method, sentence: reading instructional method presenting whole sentences as thought units rather than first presenting letters or words or phrases

method, sight: reading instructional method where new words are presented as complete units rather than as letters or phonemic elements; look-and-say method

method, SQ3R: survey, question, read, recite (to self), review; a reading-study method initiated by Francis P. Robinson which can be applied to an assigned selection or a whole chapter

method, synthetic: reading instructional method in which the learner starts with short and simple units such as letters of the alphabet, syllables, etc., and progresses to polysyllabic words, phrases, and sentences; part-to-whole, as in the Lippincott program

method, whole word: see method, sight

method, word picture: see clue, picture

MF: available in microfiche, as indicated in ERIC publications such as RIE (q.v.)

microcephalia: having an abnormally small head

microfiche: small 4" x 6" card (negative) which can be placed in a magnifying reader; contains the equivalent of several pages of a book or a whole journal article

microfilm: negative photograph on film, miniature in size, to be projected on a screen for reading

midline: the median line or median plane of the body; laterality development is in reference to the median plane

Miles Peep-Hole method: see method, Miles Peep Hole

minimal brain dysfunction: a mild neurological abnormality causing learning difficulties in a child with normal or near-normal intelligence

minimal pair: two utterances distinguished by a single contrast, as *fat/sat,* or *He's here/He's here?*

minor premise: in a syllogism, the second proposition which introduces the minor term

mirror reading: see reading, mirror

mirror writing: see writing, mirror

miscue: erroneous response to written language resulting from the reader's grammatical system interacting with his experience with the environment and the printed page

mixed cerebral dominance: theory that speech or language disorders may be due wholly or partly to the fact that one cerebral hemisphere does not consistently lead the other in control of bodily movement

mixed dextral: person who is right-handed and left-eyed

mixed laterality, or lateral confusion: tendency to perform some acts with a right side preference and others with a left, or the shifting from right to left in differing situations

mixed sinistral: individual who is left-handed and right-eyed

mnemonics: pertaining to memory or the improvement of memory

modal: auxiliary verbs such as *can, shall,* and *may* and their past tense forms; pertaining to the mode (q.v.)

modal age: chronological age that is most typical of children within a grade

modal-age norms: norms based only on pupils near the modal age for their actual grade placement; used on most school-level achievement batteries in establishing grade-placement scores

modality: group of common sensory qualities which form a pathway for receiving information and learning, as the visual modality, auditory modality, etc.; most children seem to prefer some modality over others in learning

mode: score or value that occurs most frequently in a distribution

model: correctly performed example; a theoretical construct of the learning process; a theoretical, organizational, or administrative pattern to be used as a guide for actual practice

modification: relationship between a term and its modifier, as in *old/man* or *sit/down*

modified macron: a diacritical mark, almost a long vowel

monocular: the use of one eye while the other eye is shut or covered

monocular regression: right to left movement of one eye (i.e., backwards movement) during reading

monograph: detailed pamphlet covering a particular topic

monohemispheric: in only one hemisphere of the brain

monosyllabic word: see word, monosyllabic

monosyllable: having one syllable or phoneme

Montessori method: developed by Marie Montessori to provide motor, sensory, and language education; motor learning is accomplished through a carefully managed environment, and didactic materials are utilized for sensory development and the teaching of language

moron: an individual with a measured IQ between 50 and 75; a high grade mental defective

morph: a word element meaning "form"

morpheme: smallest meaning-bearing unit in the structure of words; a root, prefix, suffix, or an inflectional ending, such as *singing* has two morphemes—*sing* and *ing*

morphology: linguistic system of meaning units in a language; the study of word formation

morphophoneme: set of phonemes that occurs within the allomorphs of a morpheme, such as the plural *s* after *bat, dog,* and *church* are */s/, /z/,* and */ez/*

motile, motor-minded: mental images triggered by feelings, actions, or movement

motivation: arousing inner stimulation to learning or action

movement, lip: extraneous movement of the lips when reading silently

movement patterns: organization of single movements into composite wholes, allowing the learner to concentrate on the goal rather than each step

movigenic theory: hypothesis concerning learning difficulties developed by Barsch, which defines movement and its connection to learning and relates movement patterns to learning efficiency, e.g., the child's infant motor development is used as a foundation for later motor activities

multiple-causation theory: a theory which states that the cause of poor reading is a group of factors

multiple-choice test: see test, recognition

multiple meanings: word with several meanings, as *run* in *he scored a run; he can run fast; she has a run in her stocking; we will run the blockade,* etc.

multiple-track plan: placing children in one of various homogeneous groups formed on the basis of intelligence and reading

muscle artifact: irregularity in EEG tracing caused by the electrical signal produced by the movement of a muscle

muscular imbalance: see imbalance, muscular

muscular imbalance, lateral: exophoria, exotropia, or esotropia (q.v. each)

muscular imbalance, vertical: hyperphoria, hypophoria, hypertropia, or hypotropia (q.v. each)

mutation: in heredity, change between one generation and the next in the hereditary pattern carried by the genes and chromosomes

mutism: the state of being unable to speak due to psychic causes or deafness

myelin: white material that surrounds the medullated nerve fibers

myelinization: the acquisition of the myelin sheath which insulates neurons; an indication of the neuron's readiness to function

myope: nearsighted individual

myopia: condition in which light rays focus ahead of the retina instead of on it; nearsightedness

Nn

N: symbol used to represent the number of individuals in the group, as N = 25

narcolepsy: condition in which individual has many uncontrollable short sleep periods

narrative material: see material, narrative

nasal: speech sound formed through the nose with the mouth closed, as /m/, /n/, /ng/

national norm: a statistical figure which represents usual performance based on a nationwide sampling

natural language: language spoken naturally by human beings, in contrast to the artificial languages of computers, mathematics, and symbolic logic

near point of accommodation: nearest point at which the eye can see an object clearly

nearsightedness: see myopia

needs: requirements that are developed within the individual and help him to adjust to the society in which he lives; there are societal needs and physiological needs which may be considered in the educational program

needs assessment: evaluation of the school population to establish instructional priorities

negativism: extreme opposition and resistance to suggestions or advice

nerve deafness: deafness caused by damage to the auditory nerve

neural: pertaining to nerves

neurasthenia: nervous disorder characterized by abnormal fatigability

neurogram: habit; automatic response

neurological examination: examination of sensory and motor responses, especially of the reflexes, to determine whether there is localized impairment of the nervous system

neurologically handicapped: child who evidences minimal impairment of neuromotor functioning

neurologist: a medical doctor who specializes in treatment of the nervous system and its disorders

neurology: branch of medical science that deals with the nervous system and its disorders

neuron: a nerve cell, including its axon and dendrites

neuropathology: disease or defect of the nervous system

neurophrenia: Doll's term for the symptoms of behavior resulting from impairment of the central nervous system

neuropsychology: study of the nervous system involved in higher mental operations such as learning and memory

neurosis: mental disorder generally of milder character than a psychosis; "phobias" and "nervous breakdown" usually refer to a neurosis

neurotology: branch of medical science dealing with the structure and functions of the internal ear and its nervous connection with the brain

neutralization: absence of a contrast between two phonemes in a particular phonological environment, e.g., $/i/$ and $/iy/$ contrast before most consonants, as in *bit* and *beat,* but not before $/r/$, so *here* may be written as either $/hir/$ or $/hiyr/$

New Castle method: see method, New Castle

Newbery Award: medal awarded annually to the author of the most distinguished contributions to American children's literature

newsprint: cheap paper made from wood pulp or recycled paper on which newspapers are printed

NIE: National Institute of Education, which designed and supports the national information system, ERIC

nondirective therapy: see therapy, nondirective

nonfiction: classification of books which are not novels or stories

nongrading: organizational plan without grade designations to which children are assigned on the basis of achievement; instruction is carried out through a planned sequence over a period of years

non-oral method: see method, non-oral

nonprofessional personnel: staff members who are not responsible for instruction of pupils, directly or indirectly

nonreader: a person who cannot read, even after considerable instruction

nonsense syllable: syllable pattern that is not used in a language but is nevertheless possible, like *boma* and *glip,* as opposed to an impossible syllable like *rlezk*

non-significant: not resulting in a difference in meaning, linguistically

nonstandard English: dialect diverging noticeably from standard dialect in pronunciation, lexicon, and/or grammar

nonverbal intelligence: see intelligence, nonverbal

nonverbal test: see test, nonverbal

norm: average, normal, or standard performance for a specified group

norm, age: norm for a given age; age equivalent for a raw-score value

norm, modal age: age score in a frequency distribution which has the greatest frequency

normal curve: see curve, normal

normal distribution: see distribution, normal

normal distribution curve: bell-shaped curve representing the theoretical distribution of an infinitely large number of scores with deviation from the mean only by chance, see Figure 1. (percentages indicate percent of total area under the curve which is within the area marked off by each standard deviation, σ)

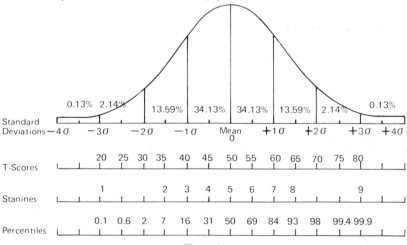

Figure 1.

normalized standard score: derived score expressed in terms of its standard deviation units from the mean and transformed to a normal distribution such as T-scores which have a mean of 50 and a standard deviation of 10

norming population: group of subjects used to establish average performance for various age or grade groups

norms: summarized values and statistics which describe the test performance of some particular group(s); common norms are age, grade, and standard score

nosographic definition: provides a description of the disorder without referring to causes

nosological definition: provides a description of the disorder as to its etiology and classification

noun: name of a person, place, or thing; their inflectional morphemes are the noun possessives and plurals, and those verbs, adjectives, etc. to which noun-forming suffixes have been added, as *slowness, tallness*

null hypothesis: in experimental studies, the fact to be tested: that there is no difference between groups or subjects greater than could be expected by chance

number concepts: ability to count and use numbers to represent quantity

nystagmus: involuntary jerky movements of the eyes

Oo

oak tag: tag board; heavy, unlined cardboard-type paper used for charts, construction art work

obesity: abnormal body fat accumulation; such overweight may have a number of causative factors other than mere caloric intake

objective test: see test, objective

objectives: specific terminal behavior desired from a learner (goal); these objectives form the basis for the development of learning strategies

obsession: persistent unwanted idea that cannot be eliminated by reasoning

occipital horn: a fluid-filled cavity forming part of the lateral ventricles within the brain's occipital lobe

occlusion: blocking or stopping an opening, such as obscuring vision

ocular: pertaining to the eye

ocular defect: see defect, ocular

ocular dominance, sighting: motor-ocular dominance in which one eye is ordinarily used in unilateral sighting

oculist: medical doctor specializing in the treatment of diseases and orders of the eye; *syn.* opthalmologist

oculomotor: having to do with movements of the eyes

oculus dexter (O.D.): right eye

oculus sinister (O.S.): left eye

oculus uterque (O.U.): both eyes

offset: method of printing in which the original copy is reproduced photographically on a metal plate, transferred to a rubber blanket, and then onto paper

omnibus test: test in which items measuring a variety of mental operations are all combined into a single sequence rather than being grouped together by type of operation; composite test

onomatopoeic words: see words, onomatopoeic

ontogeny: life cycle of an individual

open shelf collection: books in a library that are directly accessible to the library users

operant behavior: self-intiated behavior whose rate or form is affected by its consequences

ophthalmic: relating to the eye

ophthalmograph: device for photographing eye movements during reading

ophthalmologist: medical doctor who treats medical and surgical problems of the eye

ophthalmology: medical specialty dealing with vision and the eye

ophthalmoscope: instrument for inspection of the interior of the eye

optic axis: line where the refracting surfaces of the eye should be centered; the central line of vision

optic chiasma: place where half the fibers of each optic nerve cross and join the other optic nerve

optician: one who makes and often dispenses eyeglasses or other optical instruments

optimum: the most favorable amount or condition

optometrist: vision specialist licensed to prescribe refractions and to treat the functional aspects of vision but who cannot use drugs or treat eye diseases as an M.D. can

oracy: communication skills of oral language such as listening and speaking

oral: pertaining to that which is spoken

oral method: see method, oral

oral reading test: see test, oral reading

organ of Corti: part of the sense organ for hearing; a structure within the cochlea containing thousands of hair cells, the receptors for hearing; each hair cell responds to specific sounds, and excitation of the hair cells in turn stimulates the nerve endings at the start of the acoustic nerve leading to the brain

organic hyperkinetic syndrome: coined by Doyle to describe a child who exhibits the following symptoms: reading disability, perceptual difficulties, hyperactivity, mixed dominance, concentration problems, moodiness, temper tantrums, antisocial behavior, low frustration tolerance, hyperthymia, poor impulse control, imbalance, and unpredictability; on tests, this child has difficulties with tasks that involve motor, visual, and auditory areas and scores higher on verbal than performance tasks

organicity: condition which has its source in central nervous system dysfunction

organismic age: see age, organismic

organismic theory: Olsen's hypothesis that reading ability is a function of the child's total development

orientation: psychological preparation for, or adjustment to, a given task or situation; spatially, the child's ability to locate himself in relation to things surrounding him

orthography: part of grammar which considers the writing of words in correct spelling order and according to proper accepted usage

orthophoria: normal condition when eye muscles are correctly balanced

orthopsychiatry: preventive psychiatry concerned especially with the study of children

orthoptics: correct eye muscle movements for complete binocular vision

ossicle: small bone; one of the chain of three small bones in the middle ear—malleus, incus, and stapes

otitis media: inflammation or fluid in the middle ear, acute or chronic; ear infection

otologist: a physician specializing in hearing defects and diseases of the ear

otology: science of the ear, its anatomy, functions, and diseases

otosclerosis: formation of spongy bone in the capsule of the labyrinth of the ear; results in deafness

out of print: no longer available from the publisher because the supply is exhausted

overcompensation: excessive effort to strengthen a trait in which one feels inferior

overconvergence: tendency of the eyes to turn inward

overlap: extent to which scores of one distribution are the same as those of another distribution, usually expressed in percent of one set which exceeds the mean of another set

overt: outward, easily observed, public

overt behavior: see behavior, overt

overtone: acoustically, a frequency higher than that of the fundamental frequency; additional meaning implied

Pp

pacer: machine with controlled exposure to reading material with the purpose of increasing reading rate, as the EDL Controlled Reader, SRA Accelerator

pacing: allowing the child to set his own rate of reading according to his ability to comprehend and his maturity in reading; given by proponents of individualized reading or the use of auto-teaching as one of their advantages

package library: collection of pamphlets and other material on a topic loaned by a library agency

pagination: sequentially numbered pages of a publication

paired associate: items presented in pairs for learning; when one item is later presented, the paired item should be recalled, as *two-pair, three-trio*

palatals: speech sounds formed between the tongue and the palate, as /g/, /q/, /sh/

palindrome: word, sentence, or number that is the same read from left or right, as *did, pap*

pamphlet: short, single publication, unbound, usually dealing with a single topic

panic: acute attack of intense, overwhelming anxiety with large degree of personality disorganization

paper hole test: see test, paper hole

paradigm: a model, a pattern, an example

paradigmatic association: association between two words of the same form class, i.e., *dog* and *cat*

paragraph analysis: act of finding the main idea of a paragraph along with appropriate supporting details

paralexia: dysfunction in comprehending cursive or manuscript words or sentences; most readily observable in transposition or substitution of letters, syllables, or words

parallax: the apparent displacement of one object or of the relative positions of two objects which occurs by looking with first one eye and then the other

parameter: descriptive statistic representative of the total population, as a mean or *standard deviation*

paranatal: connected with or occurring during the birth process

paranoia: rare, slow-developing psychotic disorder characterized by delusions of persecution and/or grandeur

paraphrasing: restating the thoughts of an author in one's own words

paraprofessionals: in teaching, individuals who are employed to assist classroom teachers but who are not themselves certificated teachers

parathyroid glands: four pea-size organs located on the lower back edge of the thyroid, the parathyroid glands secrete a hormone, parathyrin, which controls the metabolism of phosphorous and calcium

paresis (pa-rē-sis): partial loss of muscular power, weakness of a limb

paroxysm: spasmodic increase in the progress of a disease; a spasm or convulsion

paroxysmal: pertaining to a paroxysm; appearance of wave patterns indicating possible epileptic discharge during brain wave tracings

participle: verb used as an adjective and usually ending in *ing* or *en*

pathodynamics: interaction of people in a group that produces disturbances in behavior or feelings; where the behavior of one member of a group influences the behavior of the others

pathological: pertaining to abnormalities and diseased conditions in organisms

pattern: consisting of regular elements which fit a specific scheme, as in the English subject-verb-object; a model or example to be imitated

patterning theory: proposed by Doman and Delacato to establish normal neurological stages of development in mentally retarded, brain injured, and other disabled children; according to the authors, among the disabled there is a breakdown in the normal progression of neurological development which can be rectified by requiring the child by himself or with adult help to go through the normal sequential stages to establish hemispheric dominance, beginning with rolling over and crawling

pause: a temporary break in an activity, such as speech; the pause in *rate table,* not in *ratable*

Pearson product moment correlation: see product moment coefficient

pedagogical: referring to the art or profession of teaching, or training for teaching

padagogy: the principles and methods of teaching

pediatrician: physician who specializes in the medical care and diseases of children

pediatrics: medical science that deals with care and diseases of children

peers: individuals of the same age, grade level, or status

percentage-correct score: derived scores indicating the individual's performance as a percentage of the total score possible; a reflection of the difficulty of the items for that individual

percentile: point in a distribution of ranked scores below which the given percent of scores fall—the 70th percentile is the point below which fall 70% of the students' scores in the distribution

perception: process by which the individual recognizes and meaningfully integrates sensory information

perception, depth: ability to judge the relative distance of objects away from an individual

perception, kinesthetic: identification of a message conveyed through touch or body movement, as tracing a word or writing a vowel

perception of position: accurate interpretation of size, location, and/or movement of an object relative to the individual observing it

perception of spatial relationships: comprehending the position of two or more objects in relation to oneself, as in s_aw

perception, visual-auditory: understanding a message which is received through both seeing and hearing stimuli, as in attending a movie

perception, word: recognizing, pronouncing, and understanding the word as a unit

perceptual constancy: accurate interpretation of a class of objects regardless of variability in size, shape, position, distance away, etc., as *car* represented by the small Volkswagen to the large Cadillac, or the words *FARM and farm*

perceptual disorder: disturbance in the interpretation of sensory stimulation from objects, relationships, or qualities

perceptually impaired: one whose learning is affected by limitations in reception of, integration of, or effective response to sensory information

perceptual-motor: the ability to receive, integrate, and respond to varied sensory input by selecting an appropriate and correctly executed motor response

perceptual-motor match: process of comparing the output data from the motor system with the input data received through perception

performance: execution of an action; actual output of speech, reading, or behavior

performance contracting: agreement between a school district and a private company wherein a stipulated sum or a per-pupil amount is to be paid to the company on the basis of measured gains of the learner or the achievement of a specified level of performance by the learner; most often used in the field of reading achievement

performance objective: learning goal stated in behavior terms that can be demonstrated and measured

performance-based: skill expressed on the basis of a performance objective

perinatal: at approximately the time of birth

periodical: magazine or journal published regularly, but not daily, such as a monthly or a quarterly

periodical index: see index, periodical

permutations: rearrangement of the order of a set of items, such as xyz into yxz, zyx, etc.

perseveration: tendency to continue a response to a stimulus after the stimulus has been removed or the response is no longer appropriate

perseveration of infantile speech: prolonging the speech habits of a 30- to 70-month-old child, beyond that time

personal reading: reading chosen voluntarily for recreation and/ or information

personality: person's mental, emotional, and temperamental make-up as they affect his personal and social relationships

personality disorders: broad term for abnormal personality structure

personality, inadequate: relative ineptness in coping with demands of daily living, poor judgment, social instability, and lack of stamina

phalanges: finger or toe bones

phenobarbital: anticonvulsant drug used to treat children with learning disabilities; has been known to cause an increase in activity of some hyperactive and lethargic children

phenotype: total interaction of genotype (q.v.) and environment; the individual's observable traits

phenylketonuria (PKU): inherited faulty metabolism resulting in accumulation of phenylpyruvic acid which may cause mental retardation

phi coefficient (ϕ): a measure of relationship when both variables are dichotomous (e.g., pass vs. fail and boys vs. girls); may be used to assess the discrimination of a test item

philology: study of language, its origin and development

philosophy of education: system of beliefs regarding educational goals and principles

phonation: laryngeal vibration in speech sounds

phone: an individual speech sound

phoneme: smallest unit of speech sound or its variants

phoneme-grapheme correspondence: relationship between a sound unit (phoneme) and its corresponding alphabetic unit (grapheme)

phonemic notation: system for recording the phonemes of a language; as the /kw/ in *queen*

phonemic principle: generalization that the sound system of a language is made up of significant contrasting phonemes, as *pin* vs. *bin*

phonemics: study of language structure in terms of its meaningful units of sound

phonetic: referring to speech sounds

phonetic features: characteristics of speech sounds such as voice, stop quality, vowel quality, and nasality

phonetic-graphic matching: the conversion of sound (auditory symbols) into written (visuomotor) alphabetical symbols; encoding

phonetic notation or system: method used to record all noticeable phonetic features

phonetic representation: pronunciation of a form

phonetic similarity: common use of at least one phonetic characteristic by two or more sounds, as /m/ and /b/ share the feature "bilabial" and /b/ and /d/ the feature "stop"

phonetic variant: one of the possible pronunciations of a phoneme; a positional variant; allophone

phonetic word: see word, phonetic

234709.

phonetics: science of speech sounds made using the larynx, tongue, and lips, and symbols for recording them

phonic analysis: identification of the sound units in an unknown word as a means of pronouncing the word

phonic approach: studying words by associating sounds with printed symbols, sound-symbol relationship

phonic generalization: rule for the pronunciation of a particular grapheme or combination of graphemes

phonic method: reading instruction through the analysis of words from their speech sounds or the development of words by combining speech sounds

phonics: simplified phonetics used to teach the recognition and pronunciation of words in reading through sound-symbol relationships

phonics, analytic (whole word): analytic method in which a specific phoneme is identified within a whole word rather than the sounding of isolated phonemes which are blended into whole words; first a series of sight words is learned, phonemes are then identified; a whole-to-part approach

phonics, cluster (units): type of synthetic phonics which deals with letter group or phonic family sounds, as /at/ in *mat, sat, bat, hat, cat*

phonics, incidental: phonics skills are taught as the pupil encounters the need for them, rather than in a structured, preplanned format

phonics, letter: synthetic type of phonics which deals with letter sounds rather than with sounds of letter groups or phonic families

phonics, synthetic: sounding words out by letter, or phonic units, and then blending the sounds; a method of instruction in beginning reading

phonogram: letter or a group of letters representing a speech sound, as /at/, /ake/

phonogram, compound: phonic unit of more than one letter which does not make a word by itself, as *ay, ing, ou*

phonogram, letter: single consonant

phonogram, word: small word (sight word, q.v.) which serves as a word element in longer words, as *an, in*

phonology: linguistic system of speech sounds in the language, its historical changes and development

phoria: the way the eyes are directed in viewing an object; see heterophoria

phoria, lateral: deviation of the eye inward or outward; see esophoria, exophoria, exotropia, esotropia

phoria, vertical: deviation of the eye upward or downward; see hyperphoria, hypophoria, hypertropia, hypotropia

photophobia: abnormal sensitivity of the eyes to light

photostat: copy reproduced directly on sensitized paper by a special camera in just a few second's time

phrase reading: reading by grouping words in phrases naturally, as opposed to word-by-word

phrase structure grammar: grammatical structure of sentences without the use of transformations

phylogenetic: characteristics of the race or species instead of that of the individual

phylogeny: evolution of the race or group of genetically related organisms

physiological measures: procedures or instruments which are used to assess physical development, ability, or capacity

Piaget: Swiss psychologist who theorized a developmental cognitive organization which includes four stages: sensory-motor operations, preoperational, concrete operations, formal operations

pica: size of type; a unit of measure in printing in which six picas equals one inch

pictograph: picture representing a word or idea; pictorial symbols that tell a story

picture book: see book, picture

picture clue: see clue, picture

picture dictionary: see dictionary, picture

pitch: lowness to highness of the voice or sound corresponding roughly to sound frequency; pitch and stress are meaning-bearing agents in speech

pituitary gland: endocrine gland situated near the base of the brain which regulates growth

play therapy: child is placed in a free play situation, usually limited only by the four walls, so that he may play (act) out his frustrations, disturbance, undesirable traits; observations by the therapist lead to diagnosis of causes for his problems

plosive: consonant produced by closing, then suddenly opening, the nasal-oral passages, as /b/ and /p/

plus lens: convex lens utilized in correcting farsightedness

plus lens test: see test, plus lens

pneumoencephalogram: X-ray taken of the ventricular spaces of the brain immediately following the injection of air or gas

pocket chart: container or holder for flash cards or sequential elements of a story, matching games, etc.

point: printer's standard measure of type size, .34 mm.; twelve points equal one pica

pointing test: see test, pointing

polyglot: characteristic of a book containing the text in several languages; speaking or writing many languages

polysyllable: a word with several syllables strung together

pons: band of nervous tissue across the upper part of the medulla oblongata

population: any entire group from which a sampling can be tested; statistical inferences are made from the sample and applied to the total group

position in space: significance is dependent on relative order and/or position, i.e., *was* vs. *saw*; *p* vs. *q*; see spatial relationships

positional variant: variant of a phoneme (allophone) or morpheme (allomorph) occurring in a specific environment; the phoneme /p/ has a /p/ allophone initially in *pat* but a /p/ allophone after /s/ in *spat*

possible word: word that conforms to the phonemic and grammatical patterns of the language but has no meaning, as *stanes* and *flark* in *Do stanes flark?*

posterior cranial fossa: lowest in position of the three cranial cavities; it lodges the cerebellum, pons, and medulla oblongata

posttest: measure taken after some procedure to evaluate the learner's change or post-instruction behavior

posturalization: term coined by Delacato describing the position of a child's head, arms, and legs during sleep

potentiality: latent power, aptitude, capacity

power, discriminating: power of a test or test item to distinguish among good and poor performers on the characteristic tested

power test: see test, power

practice effect: influence of previous experience on the later performance of the same or a similar task, often applied to test-retest situations

practice or drill: repetition of a learning experience to aid in retention of skills or knowledge or to make the desired response an habitual one

praxis: practice or performance of a skill

precis (prā-sē): brief summary of a book or article

preconceived idea: predetermined point of view unmodified by the introduction of new and relevant concepts; a prejudgment

predicate phrase: part of a sentence containing the verb and any of its complements

predication: relationship between a subject noun phrase and a predicate phrase, as *Jack/came*

preface: note preceding the text of a book usually containing the purpose and scope of the book and sometimes acknowledgments; differs from introduction

preferred eye: see eye, preferred

prefix: affix placed before the morpheme(s) of a word that changes or modifies the meaning, as */dis/* in *dislike* and */sub/* in *sublease*

premise: proposition or basis on which a conclusion or further reasoning may be drawn; one of the two propositions of a syllogism (q.v.)

prenatal: pertaining to the time during pregnancy before birth

preprimer: booklets containing the first stories of a basal reader series, used after readiness materials and before the *Primer*; most of them contain pictures and a limited number of new words with considerable repetition

prerequisite: knowledge and abilities that the individual must have mastered before proceeding to a new task

presbyopia: defect of vision due to loss of elasticity of the crystalline lens with age; near objects are seen with difficulty

prescriptivism: doctrine that part of the grammarian's task is to prescribe good usage (a set of rules) in order to improve the language

pretest: measure for evaluating the learner's behavior or knowledge status before the instructional program begins

preview: act of making a temporary initial survey of a selection, chapter, or book

primary accent: see accent, primary

primary cause: see cause, primary

primary motor strip: section of the frontal lobe, also called precentral gyrus of the brain, which controls motor activity

primary reading retardation: see reading retardation, primary

primary, ungraded: school organizational plan for breaking the primary grades (1-3) into shorter steps approaching continuous progress; the child is not formally promoted until he completes the program, whether it be 2, 3, or 4 years

primer: "first book" in a reading series, although it is typically preceded by readiness and *preprimers*; consists of about 120-150 pages, containing gradually introduced new words as well as words learned from the previous booklets and materials

principle: generalization based on accumulated facts or observations

probable error (P.E.): measure of variability, used infrequently today, obtained by multiplying the standard error or standard deviation by .6745; in a normal distribution, one-half of the cases lie with $\pm$ 1 P.E. of the mean

process skills: subskills necessary to perform a higher level task

product moment coefficient: widely used correlation coefficient indicates linear relationships; Pearson product moment coefficient of correlation symbolized by r:

$$r = \frac{\Sigma xy}{N\sigma_x\sigma_y}$$

productive inflection: inflection used for newly coined words

professional personnel: school staff members who are directly or indirectly responsible for the learning program of pupils

proficiency: degree or level of ability currently demonstrated

profile: graphic representation of an individual's traits or performance scores on tests

prognosis: forecast or prediction of future condition or success

program: body of subjects and/or learning experiences that make up the curriculum; the subject matter that is to be learned by the student via a machine or other device

program, balanced reading: an instructional design providing a balance between study-type reading, recreational reading, oral reading, and silent reading

program, basal-reading: instructional reading program which is designed to teach the basic reading skills through the use of a sequentially developed set of prepared reading materials

program, experience–unit: program in which different reading materials are gathered and centered around a common theme or unit of child experiences

programmed learning: lesson(s) provided in progressive easy steps for auto-instruction, requiring the learner to respond at each step with answers following each item; may be in book, sheet, or machine presentation

programming: process of preparing the material to be learned in a series of short sequential steps; usually moving the student from a familiar to a more complex set of concepts and principles

progress chart: see chart, progress

projection: ego defense mechanism in which the individual places the blame for his difficulties upon others or ascribes to others his own experiences or feelings

projection rules: set of rules for combining the meanings of the individual words into a probable meaning for the whole sentence

projective technique: method of personality measurement which makes use of deliberately ambiguous stimuli such as ink blots, incomplete sentences, picture situations, clouds, etc., into which the individual "projects" manifestations of his personality characteristics

projective test: see test, projective

projector: optical device which projects an enlarged image on a screen, thus allowing viewing by a group

pronominal: word which can replace a noun phrase, as *the little girl/came; she/came*

pronominalization: transformation that substitutes a pronominal for a noun phrase: *Bill cut Bill* is pronominalized to *Bill cut himself* if only one person is involved

pronunciation: utterance of the sounds of words

proofreading: meticulous reading of the printer's copy for the purpose of identifying errors which are then indicated through the use of proof marks

prophylaxis: a preventive measure

proprioceptor: sense organs of the inner ear, the semicircular ear canals, and muscles, tendons, and joints which are sensitive to the position and movement of the body

prospectus: pamphlet advertising a new publication or business

protagonist: the leader in an activity or contest

proximo-distal: from center outward, as movement of the large muscle group lying toward the center of the body develops before independent movements of parts lying at the extremes; movements of total leg precede those of ankle and toes

pseudonym: author's assumed name to hide his true identity

psychiatry: medical science that deals with the origin, prevention, diagnosis, and treatment of mental and emotional disorders; the psychiatrist is a medical doctor

psychodrama: therapeutic technique in which a patient spontaneously acts out disturbing situations typical of those causing him anxiety, thus furnishing the therapist with insight

psychoeducational diagnostician: specialist who diagnoses and evaluates a child who is having difficulty in learning, using a variety of psychological and educational testing instruments

psycholinguistics: an area of common concern in psychology and linguistics studying how individuals learn and use language, the resultant blend allows the examination of language as a total process

psychological measures: procedures or instruments used to assess mental ability and personality structure

psychology: science that deals with mental processes and with the interaction of organisms and their environment; branches include abnormal, animal, clinical, educational, genetic, industrial, physiological, and social psychology

psychometrics: science of the development, administration, and interpretation of psychological tests

psychometrist: individual trained in administering and interpreting psychological tests

psychomotor: domain which includes manipulative skills, motor skills, and acts requiring neuromuscular coordination classified in the *Taxonomy** as reflex movements, basic-fundamental movements, perceptual abilities, physical abilities, skilled movements, and non-discursive communication

psychoneurology: area of study that deals with the behavioral disorders associated with brain dysfunctions in human beings

psychosexual differentiation: process whereby sexual identity is established; in humans, this differentiation is minimal at birth and is dependent on life experience in childhood for its development

psychosis: relatively severe mental disease in which there is loss of, or disorder in, mental processes

psychosomatic: bodily conditions and variations as they relate to the psychic or emotional state of the individual

psychotherapy: use of psychological techniques in the treatment of psychological abnormalities and disorders

psychotropic (drug): has an effect on psychic (mental) function, behavior, and experience

punched-hole: a system of machine-scoring tests; uses holes punched into cards, as in IBM cards

pupil: visually, the opening at the center of the iris which allows the transmission of light; a boy or girl in elementary school

pursuit movements: see eye movements, pursuit

---

*Anita J. Harrow, *A Taxonomy of Psychomotor Domain,* New York: David McKay Company, Inc., 1972, p. 2

Qq

quadrant: one of the four areas in which the visual field is divided according to a right-left and upper-lower ordering; quarter of a circle

quartile: one of three points, Q1, Q2 (median), Q3, in an ordered series of scores which divide the frequency distribution into four equal parts

quartile deviation: see deviation, quartile

quotient, achievement: ratio of actual accomplishment (as measured by an achievement test) to mental maturity (as measured by a test of mental ability); also called discrepancy technique

quotient, educational (EQ): ratio used to determine whether an individual's achievement is at, above, or below average for students of his age

$$EQ = \frac{EA}{CA} \times 100$$

when: EA = Education Age from an achievement test battery and
CA = Chronological Age

quotient, reading (RQ): ratio between reading age and mental age; the ratio between reading age and an age assumed to be an index of capacity

$$RQ = \frac{RA}{MA} \times 100$$

when: RA = Reading age from a reading test and
MA = Mental age on an intelligence test

Rr

r: symbol for Pearson product-moment correlation coefficient (q.v.)

Rabinovitch-Ingram syndrome of primary retardation: characteristics that describe children with primary disabilities; these include retardation in reading and other operational processes, auditory and/or visual perception dysfunctions, expressed language deficits, conceptualization deficiencies that are related to distance, time, quantity, and space, and body image difficulties

random errors: generally inconsistent responses which represent no particular pattern; wild guessing; children who have not had systematic instruction in word analysis making erratic responses to words

random sample: sample drawn from a population (q.v.) in such a manner that each member has an equal chance of being selected; an unbiased sample yielding statistics representative of the whole population

range: difference in score values between the highest and lowest in a distribution

rank-order correlation (rho, ρ): method of obtaining a correlation coefficient by assigning ranks to each score of all individuals and determining the relationship between them

rapport: a mutually harmonious relationship

rate of comprehension: see reading, rate of comprehension

rate of reading: see reading, rate of comprehension

ratio IQ: derived score found by the formula: 100 (MA/CA), where
MA = mental age determined from a test and
CA = chronological age

ratio, type-token: computed by dividing the total number of running words (tokens) into the number of different words (types)

rationalization: attempt to justify a position or action that is not justifiable by giving a (different) socially acceptable reason

raw score: see score, raw

readability: measure of the difficulty or complexity of any printed material; various formulas are used to identify this difficulty, but all formulas generally include the number of words per sentence, the number of words not on a general list and therefore defined as unfamiliar, and sentence length; cloze technique is a promising new technique

readability formula: see formula, readability

readability level: indication of the difficulty of reading material in terms of the grade level at which it might be expected to be read easily

reader, corrective: student whose skills are generally near grade level but who has a specific area which is deficient; such a student can become generally deficient if enough specific areas are not improved; such activity can be executed generally within the classroom framework

reader, developmental: a child who is at or near expectancy for age or grade, receiving a planned program of diversified reading designed to reach the goal of a balanced reader

reader, disabled: see reader, retarded

reader, graded: reading textbook appropriate for a given level

reader, remedial: degree of deficiency differs from school to school but usually the child experiences a generalized skill deficiency requiring a detailed diagnosis and prescription for treatment outside the classroom

reader, retarded: child who is functioning below his expectancy level in one or more reading skills; degree of deficiency varies relative to the local school situation; with norms appropriate to the population involved, one year below grade in primary and two years or more in grades above the primary is considered retarded (in reading); *syn.*, disabled reader; specific types, see reader, corrective and reader, remedial

reader, supplementary: book that extends the reading experiences of the pupil at a given grade level; it may be the same or slightly more difficult than the basal reader

Readers' Guide to Periodical Literature: an index to magazine and journal articles

109

readiness: period of reading instruction that precedes the formal reading instruction; emphasizes the development of the prerequisities to successful reading achievement at any level; reading readiness (q.v.)

readiness, conceptual: child's maturational level of development in dealing with abstract concepts

reading: process of securing meaning from symbols; a physical, mental, psychological activity composed of acts of identifying, interpreting, and evaluating messages conveyed through the medium of printed symbols

reading age: see age, reading

reading, audience: individual or group reading orally to a *listening* audience

reading clinic: see clinic, reading

reading clinician: one who provides diagnosis, remediation, or the planning of remediation for the more complex and severe reading disability cases; must meet the qualifications as stipulated for the special teacher of reading (q.v.) and complete a sixth year of graduate work including (1) an advanced course(s) in the diagnosis and remediation of reading and learning problems (2) a course(s) in individual testing (3) an advanced clinical or laboratory practicum in the diagnosis and remediation of reading difficulties (4) field experiences under the direction of a qualified reading clinician (as per The Professional Standards and Ethics Committee of the IRA)

reading club: group which meets periodically with a librarian or teacher to discuss books

reading comprehension: ability to understand, recall, and paraphrase what has been read

reading consultant: works directly with teachers, administrators, and other professionals within a school to develop and implement the reading program under the direction of a supervisor with special training in reading; must meet the qualifications as stipulated for the special teacher of reading (q.v.) and complete, in addition, a sixth year of graduate work including (1) an advanced course in the remediation and diagnosis of reading and learning problems (2) an advanced course in the developmental aspects of a reading program (3) a course(s) in curriculum development and supervision (4) a course and/or experience in public relations (5) field experiences under a qualified reading consultant or supervisor in a school setting (as per The Professional Standards and Ethics Committee of the IRA)

reading, content: reading of informational materials that are part of the curriculum (science, social science, mathematics, etc.) as contrasted with reading narrative materials for recreational purposes

reading, corrective: classroom instruction designed to meet the needs of students who, although generally near grade level, have a specific skill deficiency which, uncorrected, could produce a generalized deficiency

reading, critical: evaluating the quality, the value, the accuracy, and the truthfulness of what is read

reading, cultural: selection(s) designed to improve reading tastes, knowledge of and sensitivity to various cultures

reading, cursory: reading to grasp only the general meaning and significance of the content

reading deficiency: specific skill inadequacy

reading, developmental: classroom instruction to improve the child's reading skills systematically in tune with the standard levels of progress of the particular school

reading disability: situation in which a child's reading level is significantly (a year or more) below his capacity level

reading, free: independent reading for pleasure or information; see reading, recreational

reading grade: grade placement; grade equivalent; a derived score given by reading tests, expressed in years and tenths of years, as 3.4 means the 4th month of the normal 10 month school year in the third grade

reading, individualized: method of teaching developmental reading through self-selection (usually of trade books), self-pacing, individual teacher-help, periodic pupil-teacher conferences, and variety of reading sources; does not rule out some group systematic instruction when needed

reading, intensive: relatively small, specific reading assignments for getting detailed information

reading laboratory: facility in which remedial, corrective, or developmental reading instruction is carried out, in contrast to a reading clinic which is generally remedial in emphasis

reading, leisure: see reading, recreational

reading level: individual's skill development at a given time relative to the norm, generally expressed in years and months

reading level, frustration: level at which the individual's oral fluency clearly breaks down, as demonstrated by excessive pronunciation errors and a commensurate reduction in comprehension; generally, at a pronunciation accuracy of 90% and comprehension of 50%

reading level, independent: level at which the individual can read orally with little pronunciation error and a high degree of comprehension; generally pronunciation accuracy is 99% and comprehension 90%

reading level, instructional: level at which the individual can, with teacher guidance and supervision, maintain oral reading fluency with a minimum of pronunciation error and a maximum of comprehension; generally, pronunciation accuracy of 95% and comprehension of 75%

reading methods: any directed reading activities; pedagogically, a complete reading instruction program for the schools: the basal reader method, the experience approach, individualized reading; a reading methods book presents all the various approaches to methodology in reading and relates them to the total curriculum

reading, mirror: condition in which an individual perceives from right to left with resulting reversals in letters and words, as *was* for *saw*

reading, programmed: systematically developed, self-paced, active student response, immediate feedback, instructional system produced in several formats—linear, small limited sequential presentation and branching large informational presentation—with multiple choice answers and a variety of delivery modes: machines, scrambled texts, single sheet, and workbook

reading quotient: see quotient, reading

reading, rate of comprehension: the speed with which the individual can read with understanding (about 80% level of comprehension with appropriate reading material); a measure of speed without a comprehension check is superfluous

reading readiness: general stage of developmental maturity at which the child can learn to read easily and efficiently; the term may be used to signify ability to begin each succeeding stage of reading development as well as for beginning reading

reading readiness test: see test, reading readiness

reading record: see record, reading

reading, recreational: reading for pleasure; child's choice of materials for enrichment or information

reading, remedial: instruction provided students with generalized reading deficiency by reading specialist outside the regular classroom; the clinical approach seeks the cause(s) of the disability and designs and conducts a program to correct or ameliorate the cause(s)

reading retardation: achievement below that of potential ability to achieve, even if achievement is at grade level

reading retardation, primary: primary reading disability; dysfunction in which the physiological mechanism for learning is not fully developed or is defective, thus producing a learning disorder or perceptual limitation; the child is generally of at least normal intelligence but is unable to learn to read efficiently; the problem is organic and may be sensory, neural, or motor in character; severe cases involving lack of understanding of words are called alexia and dyslexia

reading retardation, secondary: secondary reading disability; dysfunction in which a child with the capacity to learn, who possesses no physiological or mental limitations, does not acquire skill mastery; the etiology is environmental and/or psychological

reading scale: see scale, reading

reading, sight: oral reading of material without previous preparation or recourse to word analysis techniques

reading, silent: reading without audible speech

reading skill: see skill, reading

reading span: recognition span; the number of figures or words that can be visually swept and recalled in a single fixation

reading, special teacher of: has major responsibility for remedial and corrective and/or developmental reading instruction; qualifications include completing at least three years of successful classroom teaching in which the teaching of reading is an important responsibility, and completing a planned program for a Master's Degree from an accredited institution with (1) a minimum of 12 semester hours in graduate level reading courses and at least one course in each of the following—foundations or survey of reading, diagnosis and correction of reading disabilities, clinical or laboratory practicum in reading (2) undergraduate or graduate level study in each of the following areas—measurement and/or evaluation, child and/or adolescent psychology, psychology (personality, learning), literature for children and/or adolescents (3) remaining portions of the program from related areas of study (as per The Professional Standards and Ethics Committee of the IRA)

reading specialist: designation of any of the special reading positions: special teacher of reading, reading clinician, reading consultant, or reading supervisor (q.v. each)

reading, subvocal: movements of the tongue, lips, or vocal chords during silent reading which slow the reading rate

reading supervisor: coordinator or director who provides leadership in all phases of the reading program of a school system; qualifications include meeting the qualifications as stipulated for the special teacher of reading (q.v.), completing in addition a sixth year program of graduate work consisting of (1) an advanced course in the developmental aspects of a reading program (2) an advanced course in the remediation and diagnosis of reading and learning problems (3) a course(s) in curriculum development and supervision (4) a course and/or experience in public relations (5) a course(s) in administrative procedures (6) field experiences under a qualified reading supervisor (as per The Professional Standards and Ethics Committee of the IRA)

reading, supplementary: reading provided to reinforce or maintain learned proficiency in the basic reading lesson

reading taste: see taste, reading

reading vocabulary: see vocabulary, reading

reading, wide: reading a variety of materials of one's own choice for one's own pleasure

reading, word-by-word: slow oral reading characterized by pauses between words, usually due to poor word recognition skills, inappropriate or nonexistent phrasing, and a feeling of insecurity

reading, work-type: reading to find information; exercises in content-study

realia (rē-āĺia): real things, objects as contrasted to abstractions, which provide a multi-sensory aid to learning

reauditorization: the ability to recall either the name or sound of a grapheme-letter

rebus story: story which has pictures replacing some of the words throughout

recall test: see test, recall

receptive language: language that is spoken or written by others and received by the individual; listening and reading

receptive skills: see skills, receptive

recode: act of changing from one code to another as changing speech into writing

recognition: act of identifying an object due to previous contact or deduction from object's characteristics

recognition test: see test, recognition

record, eye-movement: film tracing eye movements during reading; a written record of fixations, eye sweep regressions during reading gathered by direct observation

record, reading: compilation of books read by an individual; a written record of grades, anecdotes, reading progress of the individual

records, anecdotal: written record of observed facts and behavior from which inferences can be drawn

recto: page on the right side of an open book with the odd numbered page, as opposed to its counterpart *verso*

recursiveness: capability of infinte expansion, as increasing the length of any sentence by adding a part, with a meaning that could be expressed in a very simple sentence

reference books: see books, reference

reference population: total population from which a sample is selected for measurement; standardization population

reflex: observable datum for which an historical or abstract explanation may be provided; the spelling *night* is a reflex of what we know to be a much different pronunciation in Middle English; involuntary body movements produced by discrete stimuli

refraction: bending of light as it passes through lenses or other translucent media; correcting optical defects by means of lenses

register: variety of a language used by a certain group; airplane pilots, TV technicians, and lawyers all use different registers of English

regression: horizontal or vertical backward movement of the eye through printed material to gain a second look

regression effect: tendency for a predicted score to be relatively nearer the mean of its series than the score from which it was predicted is to the mean of its series; tendency for a retest score to be closer to the mean than the pretest score

regression frequency: see frequency, regression

regressive: backward

regular: conforming to the general pattern: *dogs* is a regular plural whereas *men* is irregular

reinforcement: technical term in learning theory indicating that learning is strengthened positively by success or reward, and negatively by a penalty for error

related practice: review of skills or vocabulary which has been presented previously in the reading lesson; workbook or worksheets correlated with the lesson

relevancy: independent reading activities that the learner considers to be worthwhile; the opposite of busy work

reliability: extent to which a test will yield the same score or nearly the same score on successive trials; expressed as a coefficient of reliability (q.v.)

reliability, alternate form: a correlation coefficient (q.v.) indicating the degree to which parallel forms of a test are consistent in their measurement

reliability, content: consistency with which a test measures what it purports to measure, usually expressed as a coefficient of reliability based on split halves or alternate forms

remedial reader: see reader, remedial

remedial reading: see reading, remedial

remedial teaching: instruction offered to a learner deficient in a skill or a subject, such as the retarded reader

rental library: library operated by a commercial agency charging a fee for books loaned; a rental collection

repression: the rejection or shutting out of awareness of a thought or memory in order to avoid distress

reprint: a new printing, usually from original plates

republication: reissue of a book, usually without any changes or with minimal change, as the updating of a chapter or two

rereading: usually oral reading of a basal story after silent reading, to prove a point, dramatize, or evaluate

resource teacher: general term for a specialist who serves as consultant to teachers by providing materials and suggesting methods for instruction

response: learner's reaction to instruction

resumé: abstract or summary of a work

retarded reader: see reader, retarded

retention: learning that fosters later recall or recognition

retina: innermost layer of the eyeball which contains the visual receptors, where light waves are converted to nerve impulses and transmitted to the brain

retinal image: see image, retinal

retinoscope: instrument which measures eye refraction

return sweep: see sweep, return

reversal: perceptual inaccuracy caused by a right to left confusion of letters and words; thus *pan* becomes *nap*

reversal, kinetic: transposition of letters in a word, as *left* for *felt*

reversal, static: confusion of single letters similar or identical in pattern but differing in spatial orientation, such as *bar* for *par*

reversal tendency: tendency to reverse letters or words while reading

rhetoric: study of the art of speaking and writing effectively

RIE Research in Education: a monthly journal published by the National Institute of Education of the Department of Health, Education, and Welfare which summarizes and indexes about 1,000 documents per month from all eighteen ERIC clearinghouses; each volume contains a main entry, subject, author, and institution or publisher of documents

right-left disorientation: inability to distinguish right from left

rigidity: maintaining an attitude or behavioral set when it is no longer appropriate; set; tendency for the muscles to become very stiff after extension

Rinne Test: see test, Rinne

Ritalin (methylphenidate): psychotropic (q.v.) drug given to children to promote cerebral control over lack of attention-concentration and hyperactivity; improves muscular coordination and may cause occasional insomnia, reduced appetite, and constipation; dosage for children usually varies from 2.5 to 20 mg two or three times per day

rolling: ability to turn one's body in a controlled manner from a supine position, with arms overhead, from back to stomach, to further develop neurophysiological control

root, word: basic word from which words are developed by the addition of prefixes, suffixes, and inflectional endings, as *joy* in *joys, joyful, enjoy*

rotation: revolving of letters within a word, as *p* for *d*

rote learning: see learning, rote

rubella: German measles; can be a serious disease causing damage to unborn children if the mother contracts it during first three months of pregnancy

rule: formal statement which relates one grammatical unit to another

running: ability to run a track or obstacle course without a change of pace to aid strength, coordination, and total psychomotor learning

running head: a line of print at the top of each page of a book, usually the chapter title

running title: title of the book repeated at the head or foot of the pages throughout

Ss

saccadic movements: jerky eye movements during reading

sample: term in statistics referring to a group drawn from a larger population to represent that population

sample, representative: small group obtained by random selection or by systematic selection, weighing factors the same as for the population; an image of the population from which the sample is obtained

sampling error: chance deviation of a measured mean from its hypothetical true value

scale, reading: reading power test; one whose content becomes increasingly more difficult as the individual progresses through it

scale, vocabulary: word test in which the items are arranged in increasing difficulty

scanning: very rapid reading to locate specific words or ideas

schedule, study: systematic arranging of an individual's time and place of study

schema: an ordered plan or structure; in written form, a schematization

schizoid: having traits of introspection, shyness, and introversion

schizophrenia: cluster of psychotic reactions representing basic disturbances in reality relationships and resulting in unusual affective, intellectual, and overt behavior

scholastic aptitude test: see test, scholastic aptitude

school phobia: unfounded fear of or aversion to attending school; generally the causative factor is emotional

schwa: the soft, unstressed vowel sound heard in unaccented syllables, such as the second /a/ in *canvas,* the /e/ in *problem*; identified by the inverted *e* (ə)

Schwabach's Test: see test, Schwabach

sclera: eyeball's tough, white supporting tissue which covers it entirely except for the area of the cornea

scope: total range of learning experiences provided in a subject or in a school program

score: credit given specific response to a test item; sum of credits obtained on all items of a specific test

score, composite: a combination of several scores often weighted through multiple regression

score, converted: test score changed to its equivalent on another scale

score, correction for guessing: a reduction for wrong answers, sometimes applied to true-false and multiple-choice tests; for dichotomy choices, often R-W

score, derived: score converted from a mark on one scale into the units of another scale, as

> Grade Placement
> Chronological Age Grade Placement
> Educational Age
> Intelligence Quotient (IQ)
> Intelligence (M.A.) Grade Placement (expectancy)
> Mental Age
> Percentile Rank
> Standard Score (Sigma score, T-score, z-score)
> Stanine

score, equated: derived standard score (q.v.) which allows comparison between tests

score, grade-placement: derived score expressed as the grade placement of those for whom a given score was typical, such as a grade placement 4.3 means that the individual scored as well as an average individual in the fourth grade third month

score, raw: original score obtained by measurement, such as number of items correct on a test

score, scaled: units used to equate scores on different tests since raw scores of those tests are not comparable; standard scores

score, standard: derived score expressed in terms of the number of standard deviation units it is from the mean, as T-score, z-score, stanine; used to compare different tests

scorer reliability: indication that test scorers will yield comparable tallies in test-retest and in a single test graded by different individuals

score-T: see T-score

seatwork: planned but unsupervised classroom work carried out by a student

secondary accent: see accent, secondary

secondary reading retardation: see reading retardation, secondary

secondary source: a publication, such as a textbook, that describes or presents information published elsewhere in an original or primary source

segmentation: analysis of language into various segments: sentences, phrases, words, syllables, phonemes; characteristic inability to complete drawing a line continuously through an intersecting point or line

self-administering test: see test, self-administering

self-concept: awareness and conception of who and what one is

self-contained classroom: one teacher instructs the same children in all or most of the subject areas—usual exceptions are art and music

self-control: ability to direct one's own activities in a socially acceptable manner; maintaining restraint over one's own impulses or emotions

self-identity: self-concept; in visuomotor training, the response to mirror image and recognition of self when called by name

self-instructional device: machine, book, or other instrument used in independent learning

self-monitoring: evaluative management of the phonetic details of speech by imitating what is heard

self-selection: allowing a child to choose his or her own books for reading; a major characteristic of individualized reading

sella turcica: bony depression at base of brain containing pituitary gland

semanteme: image or idea word; the element of a word indicating its general meaning

semantic properties: component meanings of a morpheme or word; parts of the meaning of *dog,* for example, are that it is "animal," "non-human," and "concrete"

semantics: study of word changes and their meanings

semi-autonomous systems concept of brain function: theory of brain function suggesting that at times a specific modality operates semi-independently; at times it is supplementary to another modality, and at other times all the modality systems function together

semi-vowel: vowel quality speech sound utilized as a consonant, as /w/ in *web* or /y/ in *yard*

sensation: response to stimulation of sense organs

sensorimotor skills: auditory, motor, and visual abilities necessary for the development of efficient language and reading competence

sensors, distal: receptors of sight and hearing which receive remote impulses; teleoreceptors

sensors, proximal: haptic receptors of touch, taste, and movement which receive impulses from direct contact

sensory-motor: applied to the combination of input sensations and output motor responses; motor function reflects sensory organ activity

sentence: word sequence for which a grammar provides structure; a noun phrase plus a verb phrase

sentence completion tests: see tests, sentence completion

sentence compounding: coupling of two or more sentences with a conjunction such as *and* or *but*

sentence meaning: see meaning, sentence

sentence method: see method, sentence

sentence pattern: structural arrangement of a sentence, as
noun + verb + noun

septicemia: systemic disease caused by microorganisms and their toxins in the blood system

sequel: literary work continuing the course of an earlier narrative

sequence: order in which learning experiences are arranged in skill development or a curriculum pattern

sequencing: process of reading or listening from first to last and left to right

sequential development: a step-by-step organizational plan whereby one skill is built upon another

sequential memory: ability to correctly recall a series, as letters in a word, words in a sentence, or a set of directions

sequential processing: placing items in serial order

service words: see words, service

set for diversity: building receptiveness in the child for the concept that symbols may represent more than one sound, as /c/ in *cent* and *cat*

sex chromatin: spot believed to represent the x chromosome occurring normally in females and abnormally in males with the xxy syndrome; does not occur in normal xy males; recognized by special staining process

short vowel: vowel that does not say its own name and cannot appear in an open syllable, as *sit, rat, rut*

sibilant: hissing or *s*-like sound, as the middle consonants in *passing, massing, fussy*

sibling: one of two or more children born at different times from the same parents; a brother or sister, but not a twin

sight method: see method, sight

sight reading: see reading, sight

sight vocabulary: see vocabulary, sight

sight word: word immediately recognized primarily by its shape or configuration

sight-saving materials: printed matter in large (24-point, or at times 32-point) type, for reading by individuals whose vision is limited

sigma (σ): Greek letter statistically used to mean "standard deviation"; capital sigma (Σ) means "the sum of"

significance of correlation: determined by computing the standard error of the coefficient (SE) and referring to a table to determine significance at the 5% or 1% level of confidence

significant: important; difference in meaning; in statistics, a difference that would happen less than 5% or 1% of the time by chance

silent letter: letter (or letters) not pronounced in a word, as the *gh* in *sight*

silent reading: see reading, silent

silent reading test: see test, silent reading

simile (sĭm´-ĭ-lē): comparison of two basically different items, connected with the word *as* or *like*, e.g., *a heart as cold as ice*

simple sentence: one with a single finite verb

sinistral: innately left-handed

skewness: statistical description of the degree to which a single-peaked or unimodal frequency curve departs from symmetry

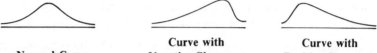

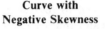

Normal Curve   **Curve with Negative Skewness**   **Curve with Positive Skewness**

skill: efficient execution of mental or physical tasks

skill grouping: arranging pupils for instruction according to specific needs

skill, reading: competency in the variables that comprise effective reading, as word analysis, con ᵣrehension, retention

skill, specialized reading: competency in the precise skill needed in content fields, as technical vocabulary of the subject

skills, dictionary: specialized skills in using the dictionary, as rapid alphabetic location of words, understanding symbols and diacritical markings, using multiple meanings correctly

skills, expressive: skills utilized in writing and speaking

skills, receptive: skills utilized in reading and listening

skimming: rapidly going over (reading) an entire passage to get a general impression or overview

skipping: to move over the surface in short gliding, alternate foot-hops with smooth coordination

slot-filler correlation: relationship between part of a linguistic structure and the type of unit that can function in that part, as a noun filling a subject function in a subject-predicate construction

slow learner: child with a measured IQ from 75 to 90

Snellen chart: a distance vision screening device with letters of varying sizes assembled on a chart used to test visual acuity; 20/20 vision represents normal vision at 20 feet

Snellen notation: ratio system for recording visual acuity in which the numerator denotes the distance from the chart and the denominator indicates the distance at which a normal eye should be able to read the test letters; 20/20 is considered normal

social acceptability: ability to get along with one's peers

social maturity: ability to assume personal and social responsibility; citizenship

social perception: ability to interpret and relate to the social environment

social skills: those abilities utilized in social problem solving and interacting with another individual or a group

social worker: person trained to help the individual improve human relationships with self, family, and community

sociodrama: dramatization and role playing used to teach understanding of one's role in society and to develop desirable social behavior

sociogram: chart which relates the relative social position of individuals in a group, usually plotted from data reflecting responses to questions regarding each person's likes, dislikes, and choices

sociology: science which deals with social organizations, social inter-relationships, and social forces

sociometry: measurement of the interpersonal relationships existing among the members of a group; as the simple sociometric method of "guess who"

sociopathic: asocial or antisocial behavior; not in conformity with society and prevailing culture; a counter-culture movement

soft neurological signs: neurological abnormalities that are mild and difficult to detect, as contrasted with the obvious neurological abnormalities, e.g., hyperactivity

somatic: pertaining to the body or body framework; used as opposite of psychogenic

sonant: voiced speech sound, as /v/, /w/

sound, medial: middle sound in a word, as /g/ in *again*

sound symbol connection: ability to associate a letter sound with a letter symbol, as associating the sounds heard at the beginning of *maid* and *mad* with the letter /m/

sound-symbol correspondence: see phoneme-grapheme correspondence

sound units: syllables

space-form blindness: condition in which a person has difficulty discriminating shapes and their relationships; space-form dysgnosia

space perception: awareness of spatial properties of an object in relation to the observer, as position, size

span, auditory memory: number of items that can be recalled immediately following hearing them being spoken

span, eye-voice: distance between the point on a printed line where the eyes are focused and the voice is orally reading

span of recognition: number of letters, symbols, digits one sees and recognizes during a single fixation

span, perceptual: number of words or figures that can be perceived in a single fixation

span, visual memory: number of items which can be recalled correctly immediately following seeing or reading them

spastic diplegia: paralysis with contracted muscles of the legs due to organic changes in infantile brain; sometimes associated with convulsion and mental deficiency

spatial relationship: an association which is based upon place or location in space

spatial-temporal translation: ability to translate relationship in space to a serial composite in time, or the reverse, as seeing a triangle and then reproducing it as a series of lines and angles

speaking vocabulary: see vocabulary, speaking

Spearman-Brown (prophecy) formula: estimate of the reliability a test has if its length is altered and other factors remain constant; usually used in correcting the split-half reliability coefficient

special service coordinator: person charged with the administrative and supervisory responsibility for the special service program of an educational agency, usually with areas of: the visually handicapped, hard-of-hearing, orthopedically handicapped, socially-emotionally maladjusted, neurologically impaired, mentally retarded, and perceptually impaired

special services: programs and services provided for exceptional children

special teacher of reading: see reading, special teacher of

specific developmental dyslexia: see specific language disability

specific language disability: specific developmental dyslexia; refers to children with adequate intelligence who have not learned to read,

126

write, spell, or communicate despite environmental opportunities and conventional instruction, although they generally succeed in science and math

speech defect: speech characterized by substitutions, omissions, distortions, and addition of speech sounds, thus interfering with efficient oral communication; defective speech

speech, delayed: speech slowed by emotional blockage, mental deficiency, hearing loss, or other factor

speech organs: lips, teeth, gums, hard palate, soft palate, tongue, and vocal cords used in speech

speed of comprehension: rate that one can read and still understand the content

speed of recognition: rate at which letters, words, or digits can be identified in a single fixation

speed reading film: an 8 mm or 16 mm moving film projected to increase the reader's rate of comprehension

speed test: see test, speed

spelling: correctly sequencing letters of a word; a form of encoding (q.v.)

spirometer: apparatus that measures amount of air which can be exhaled from the lungs after complete inhalation; used to determine vital capacity

splenium: rear part of the corpus callosum; fibers uniting the two halves of the cerebrum

splinter skill: isolated and restricted approach to a specific problem, often memorized, with no further application and thus often confusing the learner, as memorization of The Declaration of Independence without understanding its meaning

split-half reliability coefficient: estimate of content reliability based on the correlation between scores on two halves of a test, usually the odd vs. even items, corrected with the Spearman-Brown prophecy formula

spotting: see scanning

squint: see strabismus

stability, emotional: see emotional stability

stammering: irregular series of hesitations or repetitions of speech; a general term for stuttering (q.v.)

standard: level of performance agreed upon by experts or established by school personnel as a goal of pupil attainment

standard deviation (SD, S, σ): a measure of the variability of scores from the mean in a frequency distribution. About two-thirds of the scores in a normal distribution fall within a range of $\pm$ σ from the mean. It is used to compute standard scores, standard error, and various tests determining statistical significance of differences. Formula:

$$\sigma = \sqrt{\frac{\Sigma d^2}{N}}$$

standard English: formal dialect spoken and written by prestige group in society

standard error (SE): estimate of what the deviation of a score would be from the "true score" if there were repeated testing; in general, the obtained score should not differ more than one SE from the true score

standard score: see score, standard

standardization: development of a standardized test involving trying out items, item analysis, validation studies, reliability studies, and obtaining norms

standardization of test battery: development of a system of derived scores from certain tests in order to compare local results with a reference population

standardization sample: the group which represents a part of the population used in norming a test

standardized test: see test, standardized

Stanger Donahue method: British system comparable to that of Gillingham (q.v.); utilizes a VAKT technique which is heavily auditory; models of letter names and sounds are traced and written in script; also included is testing for dominance

stanine: normalized standard score of nine units 1 to 9; in a normal distribution, stanines have a mean of 5.0 and a standard deviation of 2; standard nines

static balance: static postural adjustment, as standing or kneeling balances

static reversal: see reversal, static

statistic: numerical value, such as the mean, standard deviation, correlation, or other measure characterizing a specific series of scores

stem: root word, or word form, from which new words are developed by the addition of inflected endings, prefixes, or suffixes (affixes)

sten: normalized standard score, similar to the stanine but having five units on either side of the mean; in a normal distribution, mean sten is 5.5 and the standard deviation is about 2; standard tens

stencil key: scoring device made for placement over an answer sheet; correct responses are visible through holes cut in the key

stereognosis: perception of objects by touch

stereograph: pair of nearly identical pictures side-by-side on a card which fuse into one picture when viewed through a stereoscope and yield the impression of depth

stereopsis: visual perception of objects in three dimensions

stereoscope: instrument with lenses through which the individual views stereographs (q.v.)

stereotype: rigidly and consistently repeated action; a rigid and biased perception

stimulus: any change in physical energy which excites a sensory receptor; is considered one factor in motivation

stimulus-response learning: repetitive type of exercises wherein the learner associates the response to a selected stimulus

stimulus-response paradigm: model based on the observation that a certain stimulus tends to be followed by a specified movement

stimulus word: word that elicits a response from the learner

stop: consonantal sound made by completely blocking the airstreams; *pail, tail, bail, dale,* and *gale* all begin with stops

story hour: regular period during which children are read to or told stories

strabismus: lack of coordination of eye muscles causing the two eyes not to focus on the same point; squint

strabismus, alternating: type of strabismus wherein either eye can maintain fixation

strabismus, convergent: esotropia; crossed eyes

strabismus, divergent: exotropia; walleyes

stratified sample: controlled sampling of some factors representative of the portion within the population as a whole, as community size (only small urban), sex (60% male, 40% female), grade (only 5th and 6th graders)

Strauss syndrome: collection of behaviors descriptive of a brain injured child whose impairment was due to something other than genetic causes; specific characteristics are hyperactivity, emotional lability, disordered perception, impulsivity, perseveration, distractibility

strephosymbolia: twisted symbols; a reversing of symbols found in children's reading and writing, especially found in those with learning disabilities, as *was* for *saw, felt* for *left*

stress: relative intensity with which a syllable is pronounced; a meaning-bearing agent along with pitch in speech

strident voice: see voice, strident

string: sequence of morphemes in a sentence

strip key: scoring key prepared in a column, which may be laid alongside a column of answers on the answer sheet or test paper

structural analysis: see analysis, structural

structured: learning material so organized that possible responses are limited; carefully and completely preplanned lesson

structuring: arranging teaching material so that the child is aware of what is expected of him; no further cueing is necessary

student: individual enrolled in a school or college

study: application of the mind (attending) to learning material for problem solving, acquiring knowledge, or skill development

study skills: abilities essential in locating, evaluating, selecting, organizing, retaining, and communicating knowledge in the subject fields; these include common skills applicable to all fields and specialized skills applicable to only a specific content

study-skills inventory: see inventory, study-skills

stupor: state wherein the individual apparently is unaware of his surroundings and unable to react to them

stuttering: speech impediment characterized by hesitations, rapid repetition of elements, and breathing or vocal muscle spasm; in speech correction practice there are three necessary qualifications: (1) no discerned physical or mental abnormalities (2) stutterer is aware of speech abnormality, and (3) stutterer tries to force correct speech

subject card: see card, subject

subject centered: instruction designed to focus on the subject being taught

subject entry: entry in a catalog under a heading indicating the subject

subjective test: see test, subjective

sublimation: unconscious mental mechanism wherein unacceptable drives are diverted into personally and socially acceptable channels

subordination: relationship between a dependent element and an independent element in a grammatical structure; in the sentence, *He was gone when I arrived,* the clause *I arrived* is subordinated to *He was gone*

subscore: score of a subsection of a test, which is added to other subscores to arrive at a total score

substitution: unconscious mental mechanism by which an unacceptable or unattainable goal, object, or emotion is replaced by one that is more acceptable or attainable; replacing a letter or word by another, obvious in oral reading; linguistically, the skill of replacing one letter element of a regular spelling pattern with another to form a new word, as *cat* to *sat, tin* to *tan*

substitution, consonant: word perception technique in which a child is taught to use a known consonant sound in combination with a known phonogram to form a new word, as the child knows the initial consonant /b/ in *bat* and the word *call,* using the /b/ with *all,* he can form the word *ball*

subtest: part of a test, developed to measure a specific subarea of what the test as a whole measures of a general area

subtopic: a subheading within an outline

subvocal reading: see reading, subvocal

suffix: letter(s) or syllable added to root word which changes or modifies the root word, as *able, or, ation, ous, ful, ly,* etc.

summary: concise review of a selection, chapter, book, or speech; an abstract

superfixes: word stress patterns which may affect meaning, but do not always, as *re-́cord* and *re-cor-́d*

supplemental instructor: individual who implements the prescriptive program developed by the child study team at the time of classification of the child, i.e., as defined in P.L. 94-124

supplementary reader: see reader, supplementary

supportive activities: those activities in the classroom which are not a part of the (reading) instruction, but which nevertheless add to the

131

learner's skills or general development as a reader, as word games available in the free-time corner

suppression: psychological blocking of the vision in one eye; conscious prevention of unacceptable overt actions, e.g., a child masking negative feelings in order to participate with his peers

suppression, monocular: lack of use of signals from one eye, although the visual mechanism is functioning

suprasegmental: pitch, stress, or pauses which are phonemically important as they influence meaning

surd: voiceless sound as /p/, /f/, /wh/; opposite of sonant

surface structure: relationships between the words of an observed sentence

survey Q3R method: see method, SQ3R

survey test: see test, survey

suspenopsia: suppression in the visual field of one eye when attention is directed to objects in the visual field of the other eye, as using a monocular telescope with both eyes open

sweep, lateral: see sweep, return

sweep, return: eye movement made in reading from the end of one line to the beginning of the next line

syllabarium: table of syllables

syllabary: writing system whose basic units are syllables

syllabic: pertaining to syllables

syllabication: syllabification; division of words into syllables (q.v.), usually to aid in pronunciation

syllable: unbroken unit of speech sound, containing one vowel sound, which may be a whole or a part of a word

syllable, closed: syllable ending with a consonant, as *sit, apt, not*

syllable, open: syllable ending in a vowel sound, as *be, they, thigh, me*

syllabus: outline or brief statement of the main points of a course of study or of a book

syllogism: a logical scheme of a formal argument, composed of the major premise (q.v.), the minor premise (q.v.), and the conclusion

Sylvian fissure: clevage between the temporal lobe and the parietal and frontal lobes of the cerebrum

symbolization: unconscious mental mechanism in which one object or idea is represented by another

symmetrical patterning: principle that languages tend to have symmetrical sound systems, as the number of voiceless stops in a language would be matched numerically by an equal number of voiced stops

sympathism: attempt to secure help in solving a problem and to avoid the responsibility for failure

synapse: site of communication between neurons; the point at which an impulse is transmitted from an axon of one neuron to a dendrite of another; a synapse is polarized, so nerve impulses are transmitted only in one direction, and is characterized by fatigability

synaptic transmission: propagation of a nervous impulse across a synapse

syndetic: entries in the catalog connected by cross referencing

syndrome: group of symptoms which characterize a particular disorder or disease

synesthesia: a secondary sensory impression accompanying an actual perception, as an impression of color aroused by a sensation of taste

synonym: word that has the same or nearly the same meaning as another word, as *big* and *large*

synopsis: brief statement reviewing a work; abstract; summary

syntagmatic association: association between two words based upon their probable co-occurence in sentences, e.g., *dog* and *bark*

syntagme: fusion; two or more linguistic signs or elements in a word or phrase

syntax: grammar; the order or arrangement of words

synthesis: combining separate sound elements into words, auditory or visual

synthetic method: see method, synthetic

system: arrangement of components designed to achieve a specific set of goals

systematic error: see error, systematic

systematic instruction: planned teaching based on mastery of an orderly sequence of skill learnings

systematic phonemes: the analysis of the phonemes of a language by a generative-transformational linguist

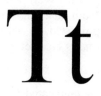

t (Student's t) test: statistical procedure for finding the significance of the difference between means of two groups, assuming a normal distribution—slightly more rigorous than the critical ratio

table: columnar listing of facts or figures for quick reference

table, age-grade: columns showing the relationship between chronological ages of pupils and the grade in which they are classified

table of contents: list of chapter titles and other parts of a book or of articles in a periodical, indicating the page on which each begins

tachistoscope: an instrument providing brief, timed exposure of visual material, such as pictures, letters, or digits; a testing or practice device for sight words or increasing span of recognition of digits, words, phrases

tachistoscope, all-purpose attachment: device which converts slide or filmstrip projectors for tachistoscopic training

tactile: referring to the sense of touch

tactile discrimination: capacity for identifying and matching objects by touch and feel

tactile perception: ability to interpret sensory stimuli that are experienced through the sense of touch

tactile procedure: tracing a word as often as is necessary to learn it, simultaneously looking at and saying the word

tactual imagery: mental reconstruction of sensory experiences obtained through touch

tactual-kinesthetic: combining sensory impressions of touch and muscle movement

tag board: see oak tag

talent: relatively high order of aptitude; capable of training to an unusually high degree

talented: young people with outstanding ability in special areas—art, music, sports

talking book: see book, talking

tapping test: see test, tapping

task analysis: examination of a particular operation or activity to determine its component elements and the processes needed to perform it

taste, reading: discrimination in selecting reading material

taxonomic phonemes: sound units of a language developed by utilizing either minimal pairs or the principles of complementary distribution (q.v.) and phonetic similarity (q.v.); this system is developed independently of the grammatic and semantic systems guided by a well-defined set of procedures

taxonomy: scientific classification of a subject area specifying its components and their relationships, as taxonomy of the cognitive domain, vertebrates, etc.

teacher's manual: lesson-by-lesson guide indicating the steps in implementing instruction in the particular material; usually containing suggestions for slower and faster students as well as average students

team learning: two children studying together

team teaching: instructional strategy in which two or more teachers with special complementary skills assume joint responsibility for the educational growth of students

technical vocabulary: see vocabulary, technical

telebinocular: mechanical device used in visual screening; measures near and far point acuity, phorias, color perception, and stereopsis

teloreceptor: sense organ which is stimulated by a distant stimulus, as eyes, nose, ears

telescoping: condensing a word to certain individual letters because of the writer's inability to see the word in its entirety, as writing *cry* for *carry*

temporal horn: fluid-filled cavity in the temporal lobes of the brain, part of the ventricular system

temporal lobe epilepsy: form of epilepsy in which the brain wave pattern caused by a seizure begins in and spreads from the temporal lobe

temporal relationship: subjects or ideas arranged in a sequence according to time

temporal reliability: test stability over a period of time, estimated through a test-retest reliability coefficient

tense: in speech, pronounced with noticeable muscular tension, as /s/ is tense, whereas /z/ is lax

terminal sound: final sound of a word; frequently referred to as the blend of a vowel with a final consonant, as *it* in *sit, ace* in *race*

test, achievement: evaluation instrument that measures the extent to which a person has acquired information or mastered skills in some area

test, associative learning: measurement of the ability to relate meaning to symbols

test, auditory discrimination: evaluation instrument designed to measure one's ability to differentiate likenesses and differences between sounds

test, battery: group of tests which have been standardized on the same population so that results on the several tests are comparable; group of tests administered at the same time

test, comprehension: measure of the student's ability to understand what he has read

test, constructed response: evaluation instrument which requires the testee to develop his answer without aid as spelling the word *cat*

test, criterion: a test whose purpose is to determine whether an individual has mastered the unit of learning

test, culture-free: general ability test that has eliminated, as much as possible, items depending upon experiences more commonly found in one culture than another

test, diagnostic: test designed to identify specific strengths and weaknesses

test, essay: test made up of open-ended questions to which the examinee writes his answers at length in essay form to be subjectively evaluated

test, group: an evaluation instrument designed to be administered to several examinees at one time

test, handedness: test designed to determine hand preference

test, individual: evaluation instrument designed to be administered to only one individual at a time, as the Stanford-Binet

test, informal: evaluation instrument developed without the use of standardization procedures and administered without set protocol; generally measures material specifically taught in a lesson or unit

test, intelligence: group or individual standardized test that measures an individual's ability to perform intellectual tasks; IQ test; test of mental ability, as the WISC (Wechsler Intelligence Scale for Children), an individual test, or the CTMM (California Test of Mental Maturity), a group test

test, language: see test, verbal

test, non-language: see test, nonverbal

test, nonverbal: a paper-and-pencil test in which the test items are symbols, figures, and pictures rather than words; instructions are given orally or in pantomime

test, objective: test scored with the use of a key identifying correct answers with no subjectivity involved; items typically are true-false, matching, and multiple-choice

test, oral reading: test in which the pupil reads aloud a selection to the examiner, who follows along marking his copy of the selection with errors such as reversals, mispronunciations, substitutions, etc.

test, paper and pencil: any test requiring no materials other than paper, pencil, and test booklet, as most group tests

test, paper hole: eye dominance test wherein the examinee sights a distant object through a hole in a piece of paper held at arm's length

test, performance: ambiguous term meaning a test involving special apparatus and minimizing verbal skills, as opposed to a paper-and pencil or verbal test, as the Arthur Point Scale or WISC Block Design subtest

test, personality: performance test, questionnaire, or other device designed to measure some affective or social characteristic of the individual

test, plus lens: 1.00 or 1.50 diopter spherical lens used to detect the presence of a significant degree of farsightedness

test, pointing: eye dominance test wherein the examinee extends an arm and an index finger pointing at a distant object; with both eyes open the dominant eye is the one lined up with the finger and object

test, power: test with no time limit measuring level of performance rather than speed of response

test, predictive: measure whose results are used to forecast degree of success or failure in future study in a specific field

test, projective: test which presents unstructured stimuli (picture situations, cloud formations, ink blots) to the examinee, allowing free response from which the clinician interprets personality traits, as TAT, Rorschach, sentence completion (q.v.)

test, readiness: test measuring the extent of maturity or the level of prerequisite skill acquisition of an individual for beginning a particular task, as beginning reading

test, reading readiness: test to determine a pupil's potential for success in learning to read

test, recall: test in which examinee must reproduce previously studied material

test, recognition: test in which several answers are given and the examinee selects the correct one, as matching or multiple-choice

test, Rinne: a test of auditory acuity which uses a tuning fork to determine which is more efficient—air or bone conduction

test, scaled: test in which the items are arranged in order of increasing difficulty or whose items are assigned values according to the difficulty of the item

test, scholastic aptitude: test of those native and acquired abilities that are needed for success in school achievement

test, Schwabach: a test of air versus bone conduction hearing using tuning forks of several frequencies

test, selected response: evaluation instrument which requires the testee to choose his answers from among several presented

test, self-administering: test with simple written directions for each part so that no guidance by the examiner is supposed to be necessary

test, sentence completion: tests presenting incomplete sentences which the individual is asked to complete immediately by providing an appropriate element

test, silent reading: group test made up of paragraphs which the testees silently read and then answer questions about; skills measured are typically rate of comprehension, vocabulary, and work study, as Gates, Iowa

test, speed: test in which performance is measured by the total items of relatively equal difficulty that are answered in a specified time

test, standardized: test composed of empirically (q.v.) chosen materials with specific directions for administration, scoring, and interpretation; provides data on reliability and validity and norms

test, subjective: test on which the personal opinion of the scorer is a determinant of the obtained score; one which does not have objective scoring standards

test, survey: test measuring general achievement in an area, concerned with breadth of coverage instead of specific details or causal factors; most frequently used for screening large groups

test, tapping: handedness test wherein the pupil taps his pencil on a sheet of blank paper for a specific length of time; tapping is more rapid by the dominant hand

test, verbal: test in which results depend on the use and comprehension of words, presented orally or visually, as in most paper-and-pencil tests

test, vocabulary: test of the number of words a person can understand, recognize, or pronounce correctly, indicated by his response to a sampling of words

test, watch-tick: rough test of hearing using a loud ticking watch which is held at varying distances from the individual's ear

test, whisper: rough test of hearing using a set of whispered words or digits

theory: a principle for which there is some substantiation

therapeutic: curing or correcting a disorder

therapy: treatment for curing or alleviating a disorder

therapy, art: use of artistic expression by the child to reflect his insights, emotional problems, mental functioning, and to provide emotional release

therapy, group: method of psychotherapy wherein a group of individuals are treated, individuals interact with one another as well as with their therapist, often gaining insight into their own problems through hearing the problems of others

therapy, language: child's free writing; furnishes insights into his emotional problems and provides him with emotional release

therapy, nondirective: psychologist Carl Rogers' form of therapy which places the responsibility for problem solving entirely on the client; clinician plays a reflective, supportive role only

thesaurus of ERIC descriptors: source volume of all subject headings used for indexing and retrieval of documents and journals in the ERIC collection; descriptors are educational terms that identify the essential content of the document

theta waves: brain wave tracings in the frequency range of 4-7 cycles per second; relatively slow waves not uncommon in children up to fourteen years, whereas a predominance of theta waves in adults is thought to be abnormal

thinking: see cognitive memory

Thorazine (chlorpromazine): major tranquilizer or antipsychotic drug that reduces motor activity and anxiety; used with some hyperkinetic children prior to Ritalin; once anxiety is reduced, Ritalin is given to increase attention span; dosage including adult range: 30-1,000 mg daily

thought question: question designed to stimulate critical thinking leading to greater understanding

threshold, auditory: see acuity, auditory

threshold of hearing: intensity of the faintest sound of any of the frequencies which can be heard in a quiet-controlled setting

thumb index: rounded notches cut in along the edge of a book identifying by letters or words the beginning of parts of the book

thyroid gland: large, ductless gland adjacent to the trachea which is essential to the regulation of body metabolism

thyroxine: hormone secreted by the thyroid gland

tic: nervous twitching of the face or head muscles, generally caused by some psychoneurotic condition but not voluntarily controllable

tilde: a diacritical mark (~) placed over a letter to indicate a palatal nasal sound, a /ñ/ in *cañon*

timbre: sound quality resulting from the pattern of overtones present which characterizes a particular sound source, such as a saxophone, and permits identifying it

time orientation: ability to judge time lapses and be aware of the concept of time

time perception: awareness of time duration, change, order, rate, in a psychological process

tinnitus (tin-nī́-tus): ringing or buzzing sound in the ears

title entry: record of a book in a catalog or bibliography filed alphabetically under the title, ignoring the article if it is the first word

title page: first page or leaf of a book including the title, author's name, and the imprint (q.v.)

T.O.: abbreviation for traditional orthography, encompassing both writing and spelling words utilizing the traditional twenty-six letter alphabet

tokens: number of running words in a unit of reading matter (originated by Dr. Wendell Johnson)

tome: large book or heavy volume, usually extensive in its coverage of the topic(s)

tone: combined intellectual and emotional effect of an individual's writing

tone interrupter: audiometer switch used to suspend the tone in order to check on subject's responses

tonometer: device for measuring pressure within the eyeball, an indication of the possibility of glaucoma

tool subject: term not in current general use meaning a subject area which practically services other subjects

topic outline: organization of main ideas in the form of headings and subheadings

topic sentence: sentence at the beginning or end of a paragraph which is the main idea or central thought of the paragraph; in beginning reading, a sentence which provides a clue to new words or to self-help exercises

topical relationship: ideas that relate to each other, making up the total

toxemia of pregnancy: type of blood poisoning associated with abnormal body chemistry during pregnancy producing symptoms such as high blood pressure, shortness of breath, albumin in the urine, and, in some instances, convulsions

tracking behavior: watching a moving object to attempt to determine or match its speed and direction

tract: pamphlet made from single folded sheets, as a religious or political tract

141

trade books: books published for general public reading, as opposed to textbooks

trainable child: one whose IQ, determined by an individual intelligence test, is 50 or less, but who may learn to perform tasks that let him become a functioning member of society

training, auditory: instruction to improve the child's skill in the perception of sound

training, visual: instruction to improve the child's skills in visual perception and binocular coordination

transcript: copy made from an original record of data or document

transfer of training: carryover of learning into a situation which differs from the original learning situation

transformation: in grammar, one of the processes wherein a deep structure is converted into a surface structure

transformational grammar: one kind of generative grammar (q.v.) beginning with a basic, simple sentence and showing a number of changes, as a word to a clause or passive to active

translator: individual who transposes the writings of one language to another language, or early language to modern form

transliteration: the characters of an alphabet representing those of another alphabet

trauma: injury caused by any physical agent; severe psychic injury

trauma, birth: see birth trauma

trial and error procedure: finding a correct solution by trying out various approaches and discarding those proving unsatisfactory

trial lessons: short lessons using visual, auditory, tactual, and combination approaches to evaluate the method by which the child learns best

trigram: combination of three letters

trigraph, consonant: combination of three consonants, as *str*

trisomy 21: Down's syndrome (q.v.) or mongolism, caused by having three instead of a pair of number 21 chromosomes

tropia: deviation of an eye from the normal position when both eyes are used; strabismus

true score: theoretical concept never obtainable in reality—an error-free score; the average of the scores obtainable if an examinee took the same test an infinte number of times

truncated: a score distribution artifically or arbitrarily cut off at some point; a distribution wherein many score at the top because the ceiling was too low is said to be truncated

T-score: standard score (q.v.) in a distribution which has a mean of fifty and a standard deviation of ten

two-point discrimination: the ability to distinguish between double simultaneous stimulation of the body surface

tympanum: ear drum

type face: the printing surface of type

type size: size of body of type given in points; twelve points equal one pica

types: number of different words in a unit of reading material (originated by Dr. Wendell Johnson)

type-token ratio: see ratio, type-token

typical-performance test: any test designed to measure what an examinee is "really like," as personality, attitude, interest, etc.; used in opposition to maximum-performance test

Uu

unaspirated: without an accompanying puff of air, as the /t/ in *stand* opposed to the aspirated /t/ of *tap*

underconvergence: tendency of the eyes to turn outward; exophoria

understandings: learnings that provide the individual with insight into a subject or skill, thus increasing his conceptual powers

ungraded primary: see primary, ungraded

ungraded program: instructional program organized by levels of learning in different content areas rather than by a graded organization

ungrammatical: not generated by the grammar and/or not produced by native speakers; these forms are usually preceded by an asterisk in linguists' writings, as *He here

unilateral: one-sided; child who is unilateral uses predominantly one side of his body

union catalog: see catalog, union

unit, meaning: the thought message conveyed by a word or expression or a part of a word (prefix or suffix)

universals: grammatical features of all languages

universe: see population

unstructured: organization and presentation of material to permit an individual freedom in response

upper case: capital letter form

urogenital: referring to urinary and sex organs

usable vision: see vision, usable

utterance: spoken sentence

VAKT: highly structured systems of teaching reading in which kinesthetic and tactile stimulation are employed in conjunction with the auditory and visual modalities; the child traces a word or letter that has been written; the most widely used VAKT systems are the Fernald (q.v.) and the Gillingham (q.v.)

validity: the degree to which a test measures what it has been designed to measure, expressed as a correlation coefficient

validity, concurrent: matching of test scores with other measures of contemporary criterion performance, as correlation of achievement test scores with school marks

validity, construct: degree to which performance on a test predicts the degree to which the individual possesses some trait or quality measured by the test

validity, content: logical evidence that the items of a test are suitable for the purpose for which the test is to be used, as in achievement tests

validity, convergent: degree to which a test shows agreement with similar or the same variables

validity, discriminant: degree to which a particular test does not overlap with variables from which it should differ, as the items of a test of mental ability and an achievement test

validity, face: acceptability of the test and test situations by the user; it appears to measure the variable as claimed

validity, predictive: how well predictions made from the test are confirmed by data collected at a later time

value judgment: ability to recognize and react to moral and ethical issues

variability: dispersion of scores in a distribution, as the spread of the scores above and below the mean

variable: anything (trait, property, or characteristic) that can change; any condition in a scientific investigation which may affect the observations made; the thing observed or measured (independent variable), and responses, as score on a test (dependent variable)

variable error: any deviation from a true score which can be assigned to one or more nonconstant influences, such as guessing, irregular testing conditions, etc.

variance: measure of variability from the mean; the square of the standard deviation

variant word: see inflected form

velum: soft palate

verb: commonly thought of as an action word; Francis* considers this definition too restrictive and submits the following: "Verbs are a class of lexical words marked by their use of four inflections: [-s] [-ed¹] [-ed²] and [ing]; by their appearance in verb phrases with certain auxiliaries, such as can, must, is, has, please, about (to), keep (on); by a small group of derivational affixes [en-] and [-ate]; by certain positions relative to clearly marked nouns; and occasionally by the superfix [∪/]

verbal expression: vocal encoding; child's ability to express himself in spoken language about items he touches and sees

verbal information: area of language which deals with facts and concepts and their skillful utilization

verbal intelligence: see intelligence, verbal

verbalism: phrases or sentences with little or no meaning; empty form of words

vernacular: language originating in the place where used; native as opposed to literary language

verso: a left-hand page of a book

vertical imbalance: see imbalance, vertical

vertical phoria: see phoria, vertical

vertigo: dizziness

vicarious experience: experience other than direct, as reading about something or viewing a film

---

*Nelson Francis, *The Structure of American English,* New York: The Ronald Press, 1958, p. 267

146

vision, alternating: condition wherein either eye can maintain fixation, the non-fixating eye experiencing suppression or inhibition

vision, binocular: both eyes acting in unison

vision, double: *syn.,* diplopia (q.v.)

vision, near point: binocular fusion at reading distance of 11 to 14 inches

vision, peripheral: visual sense outside the central area (fovea) of the retina

vision screening: sampling of visual skills to determine possible problems

vision, usable: efficiency of either eye when both eyes are seeing

visual: referring to the use of the eyes

visual acuity: keenness of vision; ability to distinguish spatial differences; efficiency level of response to visual stimulus

visual association: visual-motor association; relationship between visual symbols and their meanings

visual-auditory perception: see perception, visual-auditory

visual closure: task in which identification of an object must be made without the presentation of the total object, as a face without eyes, nose, and mouth or a clock with only numbers, no hands

visual coordination and pursuit: the capacity to effectively synchronize eye movements in following and tracking moving objects

visual defect: impairment of vision

visual discrimination: ability to see likenesses and differences in shape and form, as in letters and words

visual efficiency: see efficiency, visual

visual figure-ground differentiation: the ability to differentiate the essential (figure) from the ground (non-essential) elements of a visual stimulus

visual form discrimination: see visual discrimination

visual imagery: mental reconstruction of sensory experiences obtained through vision

visual-motor coordination: ability to relate vision with the movements of the body or its parts

visual-motor fine muscle coordination: coordination of fine muscles, as the eye and hand

visual-motor integration: effective interaction of visual-motor skills in complex situations

visual-motor memory: capacity to reproduce in motor form previous visual experiences

visual-motor spatial-form manipulation: capacity for spatial movement involving manipulation of three-dimensional objects

visual-motor speed of learning: capacity to acquire visual motor skills through repetition

visual perception: identification, organization, and interpretation of stimuli whose input is through the eye

visual reception: visual decoding; one's ability to understand or interpret stimuli, such as symbols, words, or pictures

visual span: *syn.,* span, perceptual (q.v.)

visual training: see training, visual

visualization: forming a clear mental image of an object not actually visible

visuoconstructional ability: in psychological testing, ability to do tasks like block-design building requiring coordinated action of the eyes and hands

vital capacity: see capacity, vital

vitreous humor: see humor, vitreous

vocabulary: words of a language; those employed by a person, class, profession, etc.; ability to understand words

vocabulary, basal-reading: the words taught in succeeding levels of the basal reading program

vocabulary, basic: minimum number of words and expressions required in a language

vocabulary, basic sight: a list of high-frequency words taught as sight words in the primary grades, as Dolch's Basic Sight Vocabulary of 220 words or the revision of the Dolch by Kucera and Francis*

vocabulary, controlled: words supposedly common to the experiences of a child which are gradually introduced to the reading activity of the basal readers

---

*H. Kucera and W.N. Francis, *Computational Analysis of Present Day American English,* Providence: Brown University Press, 1967

vocabulary, developmental: basic words consistent with frequency and content for the specific grade and verbal levels

vocabulary entry: see entry, vocabulary

vocabulary, listening: number of words which the individual hears and understands

vocabulary lists: lists of words, based on word count, which indicate the most commonly used words in reading and writing*

vocabulary, meaning: words for which an individual knows the meaning

vocabulary, reading: words identified and understood either in a verbal context or in isolation

vocabulary scale: see scale, vocabulary

vocabulary, sight: words that are memorized or recognized as wholes, without word analysis

vocabulary, speaking: words utilized correctly in the individual's oral expression

vocabulary, spelling: words with correct sequence of letters an individual writes or spells orally

vocabulary, technical: words used in a content field, as history, mathematics, or the various sciences

vocabulary test: see test, vocabulary

vocabulary, writing: words that the individual uses in spontaneous writing

vocal: sounds of speech or music

vocalization: undesirable movement of lips, tongue, or vocal cords during silent reading

vocational education: program of courses designed to prepare a person for a specific job classification

voiced: produced by vibration of vocal cords, as initial sounds in *big* and *those*

voiced consonant: see consonant, voiced

voiced sounds: phonetic sounds causing vocal cords to draw together and vibrate

---

*Albert J. Harris and Milton D. Jacobson, *Basic Elementary Reading Vocabularies,* New York: The Macmillan Co., 1972

voiceless, consonant: see consonant, voiceless

voiceless sounds: phonetic sounds causing vocal cords to remain open so that they will not vibrate; surd (q.v.)

voice, strident: harsh, usually high-pitched voice

volition: decision or choice of voluntary action

volubility: overproductivity in speech

volume: in the bibliographical sense, a book distinguished from others or from divisions of the same work; any printed or processed word

vowel: single open vocal sound with no stoppage, as $/a/$, $/e/$, $/i/$, $/o/$, $/u/$ and $/y/$ or $/w/$; e.g., the $/w/$ as in the vowel diphthong in *how* and *crowd*

vowel digraph: see digraph, vowel

vowel glide: a transitional sound produced when the vocal organs shift from one sound to the articulation of another

vowel reduction: change in vowel quality in situations, as under weak stress

vowel, unglided: one which sounds in unaccented syllables, such as the schwa

walking beam: two-by-four of varied length placed approximately two inches above the ground; used to develop the child's balance and laterality

Wassermann reaction: blood test for diagnosis of syphilis

watch-tick test: see test, watch-tick

weight age: see age, weight

weighting: determination of relative influence each element of a total score merits

well-formed: capable of structural description

wheel, word: a device composed of two concentric circles containing word elements used to provide repetitive practice in vocabulary or word analysis skills

whisper test: see test, whisper

whole word method: see method, sight

wide reading: see reading, wide

word: morpheme(s) regarded as a pronounceable, meaningful unit

word analysis: see analysis, word

word attack skills: see analysis, word

word bank: originally Betts' term for words in print which an individual knows at sight; currently a file box in which child stores words by letters or categories, as in the language experience approach or VAKT technique

word blindness: lack of ability to interpret words, which may be congenital or acquired; alexia

word boundary: pause marking the end of a word

word-by-word reading: see reading, word-by-word

word caller: a reader who pronounces words one-by-one instead of grouping them by meaningful phrases; may or may not understand the passage

word comprehension: see comprehension, word

word count: frequency of occurrence of a word in a given number of running words; used in formulas for readability and for regulating the number of new words and providing repetition practice in basal readers

word discrimination: see discrimination, word

word family: see family, word

word form: see configuration

word, key: word providing the major clue to meaning of the sentence

word meaning: concept associated with any particular label; as the four-legged, hairy, meowing, domestic pet is usually labeled *cat*

word, monosyllabic: a one-syllable word, as *rut*

word, onomatopoeic: word that imitates the natural sound associated with it, such as *buzz, bang*

word perception: see perception, word

word, phonetic: one that is pronounced according to phonetic principles

word phonogram: see phonogram, word

word picture method: see method, word picture

word, polysyllabic: word having two or more syllables, as *welcome*

word recognition: process of identifying and understanding words

word root: see root, word

word, service: common, high-frequency word, as Dolch's basic sight vocabulary, Kucera-Francis word list; see also vocabulary, basic sight

word, sight: word immediately recognized without the need for word analysis techniques

word, structure: shows relationship between parts of the sentence as opposed to content words, as prepositions, conjunctions, modal and auxiliary verbs, and articles

word, variant: see inflected form

word wheel: see wheel, word

workbook: book designed as a reinforcing and skill-developing tool, often used as related reading with basal readers

W.P.M.: words per minute, average rate an individual reads

writing: ability to express oneself through written language; an expressive language act; capacity to express oneself on paper; the act of constructing graphemes

writing, cursive: longhand or script writing with letters joined

writing, horizontal: system of graphemes moving from left-to-right as in English or right-to-left as in Hebrew

writing, manuscript: printing or lettering by freehand; letters are not usually connected; used in primary grades by teachers and pupils

writing, mirror: writing words or numbers backward as would be read in a mirror

writing, vertical: system of writing from top to bottom of the page, as in Japanese

writing vocabulary: see vocabulary, writing

Xx Yy Zz

z-score: see score, standard

APPENDIX A
The ERIC Clearinghouses

Adult Education
Syracuse University, Syracuse, New York 13210

Counseling and Personnel Services
University of Michigan, Ann Arbor, Michigan 48104

Urban Disadvantaged
Columbia University, New York, New York 10027

Early Childhood Education
University of Illinois, Urbana, Illinois 61801

Educational Management
University of Oregon, Eugene, Oregon 97403

Educational Media and Technology
Stanford University, Stanford, California 94305

Exceptional Children
Council for Exceptional Children, Arlington, Virginia 22210

Higher Education
The George Washington University, Washington, D.C. 20006

Junior Colleges
University of California at Los Angeles, Los Angeles, California 90024

Languages and Linguistics
Modern Language Association, New York, New York 10011

Library and Information Sciences
American Society for Information Science, Washington, D.C. 20036

Reading and Communication Skills
National Council of Teachers of English, Urbana, Illinois 61801

Rural Education and Small Schools
New Mexico State University, Las Cruces, New Mexico 88001

Science, Mathematics, and Environmental Education
Ohio State University, Columbus, Ohio 43221

Social Studies/Social Science Education
University of Colorado, Boulder, Colorado 80302

Teacher Education
American Association of Colleges for Teacher Education, Washington, D.C. 20036

Tests, Measurement, and Evaluation
Educational Testing Service, Princeton, New Jersey 08540

Vocational and Technical Education
Ohio State University, Columbus, Ohio 43221

APPENDIX B
List of Sources

1. Academic Therapy Publications
   20 Commercial Boulevard, Novato, California 94947

2. Allied Education Council
   P.O. Box 78, Galien, Michigan 49113

3. Allyn & Bacon
   470 Atlantic Avenue, Boston, Massachusetts 02210

4. American Book Co., A Division of Litton Education Publishers, Inc.
   450 W. 33rd Street, New York, New York 10001

5. American Council on Education
   1785 Massachusetts Avenue, N.W., Washington, D.C. 20036

6. American Education Publications - A Xerox Company
   55 High Street, Middletown, Connecticut 06457

7. American Guidance Service, Inc. (AGS)
   Publishers Building, Circle Pines, Minnesota 55014

8. American Library Association
   50 East Huron Street, Chicago, Illinois 60611

9. American Optical Company
   Southbridge, Massachusetts 01550

10. Ann Arbor Publishers
    Campus Village Arcade, 611 Church Street, Ann Arbor, Michigan 48104

11. Appleton-Century-Crofts
    440 Park Avenue South, New York, New York 10016

12. Arrow Book Club (Scholastic Book Services)
    50 W. 44th Street, New York, New York 10036

13. Bantam Books, Inc.
    666 Fifth Avenue, New York, New York 10019

14. Barnell-Loft
    111 South Centre Avenue, Rockville Centre, New York 11571

15. Basic Books, Inc.
    404 Park Avenue South, New York, New York 10016

16. Bausch & Lomb Optical Co.
    Rochester, New York 14602

17. Beckley-Cardy
    1900 N. Narragansett, Chicago, Illinois 60639

18. Behavioral Research Laboratories
    P.O. Box 577, Palo Alto, California 94302

19. Bell and Howell
    7100 McCormick Road, Chicago, Illinois 60645

20. Benefic Press
    10300 W. Roosevelt Road, Westchester, Illinois 60153

21. Bobbs-Merrill Company
    4300 W. 62nd Street, Indianapolis, Indiana 46206

22. Borg-Warner Educational Systems, A Division of Borg-Warner Corp.
    7450 N. Natchez Avenue, Niles, Illinois 60648

Sources (Continued)

23. Bowker, R.R., Company
    1180 Avenue of the Americas, New York, New York 10036

24. Bowmar Publishing
    622 Rodier Drive, Glendale, California 91201

25. William C. Brown Co. Publishers
    135 S. Locust Street, Dubuque, Iowa 52001

26. Burgess Publishing Co.
    426 S. 6th Street, Minneapolis, Minnesota 55415

27. California Test Bureau, A Division of McGraw-Hill Book Company
    Del-Monte Research Park, Monterey, California 93940

28. Center for Programmed Instruction
    365 West End Avenue, New York, New York 10025

29. Chandler Publishing
    124 Spear Street, San Francisco, California 94105

30. Childrens Press, Inc.
    Jackson Boulevard and Racine Avenue, Chicago, Illinois 60607

31. Clinical Psychology Publishing Co., Inc.
    4 Conant Square, Brandon, Vermont 05733

32. Committee on Diagnostic Reading Tests, Inc.
    Mountain Home, North Carolina

33. Consulting Psychologists Press
    577 College Avenue, Palo Alto, California 94306

34. Continental Press, Inc.
    Elizabethtown, Pennsylvania 17022

35. Council for Exceptional Children
    Jefferson Plaza Office Building, One Suite 900, 1411 S. Jefferson Davis
    Highway, Arlington, Virginia 22202

36. Coward-McCann, Inc.
    210 Madison Avenue South, New York, New York 10016

37. Craig Corp.
    3410 S. LaCienega Boulevard, Los Angeles, California 90016

38. Crowell, Thomas Y., Company
    201 Park Avenue South, New York, New York 10003

39. Cuisenaire Company of America, Inc.
    12 Church Street, New Rochelle, New York 10850

40. Developmental Learning Materials
    3505 N. Ashland Avenue, Chicago, Illinois 60657

41. Dimensions Publishing Co.
    Box 4221, San Rafael, California 94903

42. Doubleday and Company
    277 Park Avenue, New York, New York 10017

43. Dover Publications
    180 Varick Street, New York, New York 10014

44. Dutton, E.P. and Co., Inc.
    201 Park Avenue South, New York, New York 10003

45. Economy Company
    1901 N. Walnut Avenue, Oklahoma City, Oklahoma 73105

157

Sources (Continued)

46. Educational Activities, Inc.
    1937 Grand Avenue, Baldwin, New York 11520

47. Educational and Psychological Associates Press
    RD 1, Box 211, Spring Hill Road, Matawan, New Jersey 07747

48. Educational Development Laboratories, A Division of McGraw-Hill
    284 Pulaski Street, Huntington, New York 11744

49. Educational Testing Service
    Princeton, New Jersey 08540

50. Educator's Publishing Service
    75 Moulton Street, Cambridge, Massachusetts 02138

51. Edukaid of Ridgewood
    1250 E. Ridgewood Avenue, Ridgewood, New Jersey 07450

52. Encyclopaedia Britannica Educational Corp.
    425 N. Michigan Avenue, Chicago, Illinois 60611

53. Essay Press
    Box 5, Planetarium Station, New York, New York 10024

54. Fearon Publishers
    2165 Park Boulevard, Palo Alto, California 94306

55. Fideler Company, The
    31 Ottowa Avenue, N.W., Grand Rapids, Michigan 49502

56. Field Educational Publications, Inc.
    3430 Sunset Avenue, Ocean, New Jersey 07712

57. Follett Educational Corp.
    1010 W. Washington Boulevard, Chicago, Illinois 60607

58. Funk and Wagnalls Company
    360 Lexington Avenue, New York, New York 10017

59. Garrard Publishing Co.
    1607 N. Market Street, Champaign, Illinois 61820

60. General Learning Corp.
    250 James Street, Morristown, New Jersey 07960

61. Ginn & Company
    125 Second Avenue, Waltham, Massachusetts 02154

62. Globe Book Co., Inc.
    175 Fifth Avenue, New York, New York 10010

63. Golden Press Educational Division
    1 W. 39th Street, New York, New York 10018

64. Government Printing Office
    Washington, D.C. 20025

65. Grosset & Dunlap
    1107 Broadway, New York, New York 10010

66. Grune & Stratton
    111 Fifth Avenue, New York, New York 10003

67. Gryphon Press
    c/o University of Nebraska Press, 135 Bancroft Hall,
    Lincoln, Nebraska 68588

68. E.M. Hale & Co.
    1201 S. Hastings Way, Eau Claire, Wisconsin 54701

Sources (Continued)

69. C.S. Hammond & Company
515 Valley Street, Maplewood, New Jersey 07040

70. Harcourt Brace Jovanovich, Inc.
757 Third Avenue, New York, New York 10017

71. Harper & Row Publishers, Inc.
49 E. 33rd Street, New York, New York 10016

72. D.C. Heath & Company
125 Spring Street, Lexington, Massachusetts 02173

73. Heritage Press
595 Madison Avenue, New York, New York 10022

74. Hoffman Information Systems, Inc.
5632 Peck Road, Arcadia, California 91006

75. Holt, Rinehart & Winston, Inc.
383 Madison Avenue, New York, New York 10017

76. Houghton Mifflin Co.
110 Tremont Street, Boston, Massachusetts 02107

77. Imperial Productions, Inc.
247 W. Court Street, Kankakee, Illinois 60901

78. Institute of Educational Research
2226 Wisconsin Avenue, N.W., Washington, D.C. 20007

79. Instructo Corporation
200 Cedar Hollow Road, Paoli, Pennsylvania 19301

80. The Instructor Publications
7 Bank Street, Danville, New York 14437

81. International Reading Association
6 Tyre Avenue, Newark, Delaware 19711

82. Jastak Associates, Inc.
1526 Gilpin Avenue, Wilmington, Delaware 19806

83. Journal of Learning Disabilities
5 N. Wabash Avenue, Chicago, Illinois 60602

84. Judy Manufacturing Company
310 N. Second Street, Minneapolis, Minnesota 55401

85. Kenworthy Educational Service
P.O. Box 3031, 138 Allen Street, Buffalo, New York 14205

86. Keystone View Company
Meadville, Pennsylvania 16335

87. Knopf, Alfred A.
501 Madison Avenue, New York, New York 10022

88. Laidlaw Brothers, A Div. of Doubleday and Co.
Thatcher & Madison Streets, River Forest, Illinois 60305

89. Learning Concepts
2501 N. Lamar, Austin, Texas 78705

90. Learning Materials, Inc.
100 E. Ohio Street, Chicago, Illinois 60611

91. Learning Research Associates
1501 Broadway, New York, New York 10036

92. J.B. Lippincott Company
E. Washington Square, Philadelphia, Pennsylvania 19105

Sources (Continued)

93. Lyons and Carnahan Educational Publishers
407 E. 25th Street, Chicago, Illinois 60616

94. Macmillan Company
866 Third Avenue, New York, New York 10022

95. Mafex Associates, Inc.
111 Barrn Avenue, Johnstown, Pennsylvania 15906

96. Maico Electronics
21 N. Third Street, Minneapolis, Minnesota 55400

97. McCormick-Mathers Publishing Company
450 W. 33rd Street, New York, New York 10001

98. McGraw-Hill Book Company
330 W. 42nd Street, New York, New York 10036

99. David McKay Co., Inc.
750 Third Avenue, New York, New York 10017

100. Melmont Publishers, Inc.
310 S. Racine Avenue, Chicago, Illinois 60607

101. Merriam, G. & C.
47 Federal Street, Springfield, Massachusetts 01101

102. Charles E. Merrill
1300 Alum Creek Drive, Columbus, Ohio 43216

103. Miami University Alumni Association
Miami University, Oxford, Ohio 45056

104. Mills Center, Inc.
1512 E. Broward Boulevard, Fort Lauderdale, Florida 33301

105. Milton Bradley Company
74 Park Street, Springfield, Massachusetts 01101

106. Motivational Research, Inc.
P.O. Box 140, McLean, Virginia 22101

107. National Council of Teachers of English
508 S. 6th Street, Champaign, Illinois 61820

108. National Education Association
1201 16th Street, N.W., Washington, D.C. 20036

109. National Reading Conference, Inc.
Reading Center, Marquette University, Milwaukee, Wisconsin 53233

110. New Century
440 Park Avenue South, New York, New York 10016

111. Noble and Noble Publishers, Inc.
750 Third Avenue, New York, New York 10017

112. Northwestern University Press
Evanston, Illinois 60201

113. Norton, W.W. and Company
55 Fifth Avenue, New York, New York 10003

114. Odyssey Press, Inc., The
55 Fifth Avenue, New York, New York 10003

115. Open Court Publishing Co.
Box 599, LaSalle, Illinois 61301

116. F.A. Owen Publishing Company
7 Bank Street, Danville, New York 14437

Sources (Continued)

117. Oxford Book Co., Inc.
71 Fifth Avenue, New York, New York 10003

118. Oxford University Press
417 Fifth Avenue, New York, New York 10016

119. Penguin Books, Inc.
3330 Clipper Mill Road, Baltimore, Maryland 21211

120. Perceptual Development Laboratories
6767 Southwest Avenue, St. Louis, Missouri 63143

121. Personnel Press, Inc. (Subsidiary of Ginn and Company)
20 Nassau Street, Princeton, New Jersey 08540

122. Phonovisual Products
Box 5625, Washington, D.C. 20016

123. Pitman Publishing Company
6 E. 46th Street, New York, New York 10017

124. Prentice-Hall, Inc.
Englewood Cliffs, New Jersey 07632

125. The Psychological Corp.
757 Third Avenue, New York, New York 10017

126. Rand McNally & Company
P.O. Box 7600, Chicago, Illinois 60680

127. Random House
201 E. 50th Street, New York, New York 10022

128. Reader's Digest Services, Educational Division
Pleasantville, New York 10570

129. Reading Institute, Inc.
116 Newbury Street, Boston, Massachusetts 02116

130. The Reading Newsreport
111 W. 42nd Street, New York, New York 10036

131. Rheem Califone
5922 Bancroft Street, Los Angeles, California 90016

132. Ronald Press Company, The
15 E. 26th Street, New York, New York 10010

133. Scholastic Magazine and Book Services
50 W. 44th Street, New York, New York 10036

134. Science Research Associates, Inc.
259 E. Erie Street, Chicago, Illinois 60611

135. Scott, Foresman & Company
1900 E. Lake Avenue, Glenview, Illinois 60025

136. Scribner's, Charles, Sons
597 Fifth Avenue, New York, New York 10017

137. Silver Burdett Company
Park Avenue & Columbia Road, Morristown, New Jersey 07960

138. Simon and Schuster, Inc.
630 Fifth Avenue, New York, New York 10020

139. The L.W. Singer Company
201 E. 50th Street, New York, New York 10022

140. Slosson Education, Inc.
140 Pine Street, East Aurora, New York 14052

Sources (Continued)

141. Society for Visual Education, Inc.
1345 Diversey Parkway, Chicago, Illinois 60614

142. Special Child Publications, Inc.
4635 Union Bay Place, N.E., Seattle, Washington 98105

143. Steck-Vaughn Company
P.O. Box 2028, Austin, Texas 78767

144. Systems for Education, Inc.
612 N. Michigan Avenue, Chicago, Illinois 60611

145. Teachers College Press, Teachers College, Columbia University
525 W. 120th Street, New York, New York 10027

146. Teachers Publishing Corp.
22 W. Putnam Avenue, Greenwich, Connecticut 06830

147. Teaching Resources
100 Boylston Street, Boston, Massachusetts 02116

148. Charles C. Thomas Publishers
327 E. Lawrence Avenue, Springfield, Illinois 62717

149. 3M Company, Visual Products Division
2501 Hudson Road, Building 220-10 W., St. Paul, Minnesota 55119

150. Tweedy Transparencies
207 Hollywood Avenue, East Orange, New Jersey 07018

151. University of Chicago Press
5750 Ellis Avenue, Chicago, Illinois 60637

152. University of Illinois Press
54 E. Gregory, Champaign, Illinois 61820

153. U.S. Department of Health, Education, and Welfare
Fourth Street and Independence Avenue, Washington, D.C. 20025

154. Vanguard Press, Inc.
424 Madison Avenue, New York, New York 10017

155. Viking Press
625 Madison Avenue, New York, New York 10022

156. Webster Division, McGraw-Hill
Princeton Road, Highstown, New Jersey 08520

157. Wenkart Publishing Company
4 Shady Hill Square, Cambridge, Massachusetts 02138

158. Western Psychological Services (WPS)
12031 Wilshire Boulevard, Los Angeles, California 90025

159. Western Publishing Education Services
1220 Mound Avenue, Racine, Wisconsin 53404

160. Winter Haven Lions Research Foundation, Inc.
Box 1112, Winter Haven, Florida 33880

161. Xerox Education Division
600 Madison Avenue, New York, New York 10022

APPENDIX C
Evaluation Instruments

The purpose of this index is to list alphabetically, by category, some tests that may be useful in evaluating learning. The description for each test is brief and the source's entry can be found by checking the specific number indicated in the list of sources, Appendix B. Readers are urged to consult the literature or O.K. Buros' Mental Measurements Yearbooks (Source 67) for complete critical reviews of the listed tests.

ACHIEVEMENT

TEST	ABILITIES MEASURED	GRADE	TYPE	SOURCE
California Achievement Tests	Reading, arithmetic, language	1-14	G	27
Comprehensive Tests of Basic Skills	Reading, language, arithmetic and study skills	2-12	G	27
Iowa Tests of Basic Skills	Language skills, arithmetic vocabulary, reading comprehension and work study skills	3-9	G	76
Metropolitan Achievement Test	Reading, arithmetic, spelling and language and content areas	1-12	G	70
Peabody Individual Achievement Test	Mathematics, reading recognition, reading comprehension, spelling, general information	K-Adult	I	7
Sequential Tests of Educational Progress	Writing, social studies, science, essay, mathematics, listening and reading	1-14	G	49
SRA Achievement Series	Arithmetic, reading and language	1-9	G	134
Stanford Achievement Tests	Spelling, arithmetic, reading and content areas	1-12	G	70
Tests of Adult Basic Education	Reading, arithmetic and language skills	Adult reading levels from 2-12	G	27
Wide Range Achievement Test	Spelling, arithmetic and word recognition	K-Adult	I/G	158

ARITHMETIC

TEST	ABILITIES MEASURED	GRADE	TYPE	SOURCE
Basic Skills in Arithmetic	Computation of whole numbers, decimals and percents	6-12	G	134
Contemporary Mathematics Test	Understanding concepts, skills in areas of number and structure and mathematical devices	3-12	G	27
Fundamental Processes in Arithmetic	Fundamental processes in whole numbers	1-8	I	21
Key Math Diagnostic Arithmetic Test	Numeration, fractions, geometry and symbols; basic processes, mental computation and reasoning; word problems, money, measurements and time	Pre-school through grade 6	I	7
Kramer Preschool Math Inventory	Counting, cardinal numbers, quantities, sequence, position, direction, geometry, measurement	ages 3-6	I	89
Prescriptive Mathematics Inventory	Analysis of the basic arithmetic skills	4-8	G	27
SRA Diagnosis Arithmetic	Criterion referenced analysis of basic arithmetic skills	1-6	I	134
Stanford Diagnostic Arithmetic Test	Counting; processes of whole numbers, fractions, percents, decimals; carrying	middle grade 2 through middle grade 8	G	70

AUDITORY

TEST	ABILITIES MEASURED	GRADE	TYPE	SOURCE
Auditory Memory Span Test	Single-syllable spoken words in progressively increasing series	ages 5-8	I	158
Auditory Sequential Memory Test	Recall of digits in progressively increasing series	ages 5-8	I	158
Brown-Carlsen Listening Comprehension Test	Immediate recall, following directions, recognition of transition, word meaning and lecture comprehension	9-Adult	G	70
Durrell Listening, Reading Series	Vocabulary and comprehension	1-9	G	70
Goldman, Fristoe, Woodcock Auditory Skills Test Battery	Speech sound discrimination under both quiet and distracting noise conditions	4 years and above	I	7
Goldman, Fristoe, Woodcock Auditory Skills Test Battery	Selective attention, diagnostic auditory discrimination, auditory memory, sound symbol	ages 3-Adult	I	82
Kindergarten Auditory Screening Test	Figure-ground, blending, discrimination	ages 5 & 6	G	57
Lindamood Auditory Conceptualization Test (LAC)	Discrimination, number and order of sound	All	I	147
Maico Audiometer	Acuity, bone and air conduction	All	I	96
Oliphant Auditory Discrimination Test	Blending	K-3	I	50
Roswell-Chall Auditory Blending Test	Oral blending of sounds in forming words	1-5	I	53
Screening Test of Auditory Perception (STAP)	Differentiate vowel sounds, initial consonant and blends; recognizing and remembering rhymes; discriminate same or different word pairs	1-6	I	1
Tenovad Test of Non-verbal Auditory Discrimination	Discriminate between pairs of tones for pitch, loudness, rhythm, duration, timbre	K-3	G/I	57
Wepman Auditory Discrimination Test	Recognition of fine differences between phonemes in English speech	ages 5-8	I	158

DIAGNOSTIC

TEST	ABILITIES MEASURED	GRADE	TYPE	SOURCE
Illinois Test of Psycho-linguistic Abilities	Auditory-vocal, visual-motor, receptive process, organizing process, expressive process, automatic level and representational level	ages 2-9	I	158
Psycho-Educational Inventory of Basic Learning Ability	Motor, visual, auditory, visual-motor, social, basic skills	preschool	I	54
Pupil Record of Educational Behavior (PREB)	Visual-motor, auditory, language, math concepts	preschool to inter-mediate	I	147
Screening Test for Identifying children with Specific Language Disability	Reading, spelling, handwriting, speaking; visual-motor, auditory memory and auditory discrimination	K-8	I	50
Woodcock-Johnson Psycho-Educational Battery	Learning aptitude, achievement, interests	preschool-adult	I	147

INTELLIGENCE

TEST	ABILITIES MEASURED	GRADE	TYPE	SOURCE
Arthur Point Scale of Performance	Non-language assessment	ages 5-15	I	125
California Test of Mental Maturity	Language and non-language	K-13	G	27
Cognitive Abilities Test	Oral vocabulary, relational concepts, multi-mental and quantitative concepts	K-3	G	76
Detroit Tests of Learning Aptitudes	General mental functioning	ages 4-Adult	I	21
Goodenough-Harris Drawing Test	Non-verbal measure of conceptual maturity	ages 4-12	G	158
Kuhlmann-Anderson Tests	Verbal and quantitative	K-12	G	121
Leiter International Performance Scale	Non-verbal intelligence	2-Adult	I	158
Lorge-Thorndike Intelligence Test	Verbal and non-verbal	3-13	G	76
McCarthy Scales of Children's Abilities	Language, perception, memory, visual-motor skills	ages 3-8½	I	125
Otis Quick-Scoring Mental Abilities	General intelligence	1-16	G	70
Primary Mental Abilities Test	Verbal meaning, number facility, spatial relations, perceptual speed and logical reasoning	K-12	G	134

INTELLIGENCE - 2

TEST	ABILITIES MEASURED	GRADE	TYPE	SOURCE
Raven Standard Progressive Matrice	Non-verbal ability to solve problems presented in abstract figures and designs	ages 5-Adult	I	158
Short Form Test of Academic Aptitude	Verbal and non-verbal	1-12	G	27
Slosson Intelligence Test	Verbal intelligence	ages 4-Adult	I	158
SRA Pictorial Reasoning Test	General learning ability independent of language and reading skills	High School & Adult	G	134
Stanford Binet Intelligence Scale, Revised	General intelligence	ages 2-Adult	I	76
Wechsler Adult Intelligence Scale	Verbal and performance abilities	ages 15 & above	I	125
Wechsler Intelligence Scale for Children, Revised	Verbal and performance abilities	ages 5-15	I	125
Wechsler Preschool and Primary Scale of Intelligence	Verbal and performance abilities	ages 4-6½	I	125

LANGUAGE AND SPEECH

TEST	ABILITIES MEASURED	GRADE	TYPE	SOURCE
Arizona Articulation Proficiency Scale, Revised	Articulation proficiency	ages 3-11	I	158
Boehm Test of Basic Concepts	Internalization of concepts of space, time, quantity, etc.	K-2	G/I	125
Carrow Elicited Language Inventory	Productive control of grammar	ages 3-6	I	89
Goldman-Fristoe Test of Articulation	Major speech sounds, initial, final and medial; sounds in sentences	ages 2 & above	I	7
Northwestern Syntax Screening Test	Comprehension and expression of spoken language	ages 4-8	I	112
Peabody Picture Vocabulary Test	Verbal ability	ages 2-6 to Adult	I	7
Picture Story Language Test	Productivity, syntax, abstract-concrete	ages 7-17	G/I	158
Preschool Language Scale	Auditory comprehension, verbal ability	preschool, primary	I	102
Test for Auditory Comprehension of Language	Comprehension of verbs and syntax; receptive language in English and and Spanish	ages 3-6	I	89
Verbal Language Development Scale	Language age	one mo. to 16 yrs.	I	158

READING - Diagnostic

TEST	ABILITIES MEASURED	GRADE	TYPE	SOURCE
Basic Sight Word Test	Knowledge of 220 high-frequency primary grade words	K-3	G/I	59
Botel Reading Inventory	Word recognition, word opposites and phonics	1-12	G/I	57
California Phonics Survey	Vowels, consonants, configuration, endings and sight words	7-College	G	27
Diagnostic Reading Scales, Revised Edition	Word recognition, oral reading and phonics	1-8	I	27
Doren Diagnostic Reading Test	Letter recognition, beginning sounds, word recognition, words within words, speech consonants, ending sounds, blending, rhyming, vowels, sight words and discriminate guessing	2-6	G	7
Durrell Analysis of Reading Difficulties	Oral reading, silent reading, listening, letter and word recognition, word analysis, spelling and handwriting	1-6	I	70
EPA Word Attack Survey	Phonic knowledge and application, structural knowledge and application	K-12	G/I	47
Gates-McKillop Reading Diagnostic Tests	Oral reading, word and phrase recognition, word analysis, auditory blending, spelling, oral vocabulary, syllabication and auditory discrimination	1-8	I	158

READING - Diagnostic - 2

TEST	ABILITIES MEASURED	GRADE	TYPE	SOURCE
Individual Reading Placement Inventory	Auditory and visual discrimination, word attack skills, vocabulary and comprehension	7-Adult	I	57
Learning Methods Test	Determines students' ability to learn new words through visual, phonic, kinesthetic or combination methods	K-3	I	104
Phonics Knowledge Survey	Phonics and structural analysis	1-6	I	145
Prescriptive Reading Inventory	Criterion referenced analysis of skills	1-6	I	27
Roswell-Chall Diagnostic Reading Test of Word Analysis Skills	Consonants, vowels and syllabication	2-6	I	53
Silent Reading Diagnostic Tests	Word recognition in isolation and context, reversible words, word analysis and blending	2-12	G	93
Slosson Oral Reading Test	Knowledge of words (pre-primer to high school) taken from basal readers	K-H.S.	I	158
SRA Diagnosis: Reading	Criterion referenced analysis of basic readings skills	1-6	I	134
Stanford Diagnostic Reading Test	Comprehension, vocabulary, auditory discrimination, syllabication, sounds, blending and rate	2-8	G	70
Woodcock Reading and Mastery Test	Letter identification, word identification, word attack, word comprehension, passage comprehension	K-12	I	82

READING - Oral

TEST	ABILITIES MEASURED	GRADE	TYPE	SOURCE
Gilmore Oral Reading	Accuracy, comprehension and rate	1-8	I	70
Gray Oral Reading Test	Accuracy	1-12	I	158

READING - Readiness

TEST	ABILITIES MEASURED	GRADE	TYPE	SOURCE
Basic Concept Inventory	Terms and concepts necessary to perform primary grade work	Pre-school through grade 3	I	57
Early Detection Inventory	Social, emotional, motor and intellectual development	Pre-school through grade.3	I	57
Harrison-Stroud Reading Readiness Profiles	Symbols, visual discrimination, context, auditory clues and letter identification	K through beginning 1st	G	76
Maturity Level for School Entrance and Reading Readiness	Body coordination, eye-hand coordination, speech and language comprehension, personal independence and social cooperation	K-1	I	7
Metropolitan Readiness Tests	Word meaning, listening, matching, alphabet recognition, number knowledge, copying and intellectual maturity	K and early 1st	G	70
Monroe Reading Aptitude Test	Visual, motor, auditory, articulation, language and foot and hand preference	K-1	G/I	76

TEST	ABILITIES MEASURED	GRADE	TYPE	SOURCE
Murphy-Durrell Reading Readiness	Phonemes, letter names and learning rate	1	G	70
Predictive Index	Identification of high risk academic failures at preschool level	ages 4 and 5	I	71
Preschool Attainment Record	Physical, social and intellectual functions	6 mos. to 7 yrs.	I	57
Preschool Inventory	Basic information and vocabulary, number concepts, concept of size, time and visual-motor function	ages 3-6	I	49
A Psychoeducational Evaluation of the Preschool Child	Physical sensory; perceptual; short-term retention; language competence and cognitive function	Pre-school	I	66
School Readiness Developmental Examination Tests	Interview, paper and pencil, right and left, visual, organization of thinking, final interview and teeth examination	ages 5-10	I	71
Tests of Basic Experiences	Language, mathematics, science, social studies and general concepts	Pre-school through 1	G	27

READING - Survey

TEST	ABILITIES MEASURED	GRADE	TYPE	SOURCE
California Reading Test	Vocabulary and reading comprehension	1-14	G	27
Cooperative English Test	Vocabulary, comprehension and speed	9-14	G	49
Developmental Reading Tests	Vocabulary and comprehension	4,5,6	G	93
Gates-MacGinitie Reading Tests	Vocabulary and comprehension	1-9	G	76
Kelley-Greene Reading Comprehension Test	Comprehension of paragraphs, ability to locate answers and ability to retain information	9-13	G	70
Nelson-Denny Reading Test, Revised Edition	Vocabulary, rate and comprehension	9-Adult	G	76
Nelson Reading Test Revised Edition	Vocabulary and comprehension	3-9	G	76
Stroud-Hieronymus Primary Reading Profiles	Aptitude for reading, auditory association, word recognition, word attack and comprehension	1-2	G	76

SOCIAL, EMOTIONAL, INTERESTS

TEST	ABILITIES MEASURED	GRADE	TYPE	SOURCE
Bender Gestalt Tests	Ability to correctly copy forms according to gestalt laws of perception and organization	ages 4 & over	I	158
Bender Visual Motor Gestalt Test for Children	Ability to correctly copy forms according to gestalt laws of perception and organization	ages 7-11	I	158
Bender Visual Motor Gestalt Test for Young Children	Ability to correctly copy forms according to gestalt laws of perception and organization	ages 5-10	I	158
California Test of Personality	Adjustment as a balance between personal and social	K-Adult through Adult	G	27
Child Behavior Rating Scale	Behavior and personality	Pre-school through grade 3	I	158
Children's Apperception Test (CAT)	Projective psychological instrument that measures personality	ages 3-10	I	158
Minnesota Percepto Diagnostic Test	Visual perception and visual motor abilities; primary, secondary and organic disorders	ages 5-16	I	158
Occupational Interest Inventory	Fields of interest, types of interests, level of interest	7-Adult	G	27
Picture Interest Inventory	Fields of interest, verbal, computational and time perspective	7-Adult	G	27
Rorschach	Projective, psychological instrument that measures personality	ages 3 & over	I	158
Thematic Apperception Test (TAT)	Projective psychological instrument that measures personality	ages 4 & over	I	158
Vineland Social Maturity Scale	Successive stages of social competence	Infancy-Maturity	I	158
What Do I Like	Preference art, music, social studies, active play, quiet play, manual arts, home arts and science	4-7	G	134

SPELLING

TEST	ABILITIES MEASURED	GRADE	TYPE	SOURCE
Gates-Russell Spelling Diagnostic Test	Oral spelling and pronunciation, auditory discrimination, letter sounds, reversals, spelling of syllables and words, spelling modalities	1-6	I	145
Lincoln Spelling Test	Accuracy of encoding	2-12	G	49

STUDY SKILLS

TEST	ABILITIES MEASURED	GRADE	TYPE	SOURCE
California Study Methods Survey	Attitudes, mechanics and planning	7-13	G	27
Watson-Glaser Critical Thinking Appraisal	Inferences, assumptions, deduction, interpretation and evaluation	9-Adult	G	70

VISUAL AND VISUAL MOTOR

TEST	ABILITIES MEASURED	GRADE	TYPE	SOURCE
Benton Visual Retention Test	Ability to draw designs from memory	ages 8 & over	I	125
Developmental Test of Visual Motor Integration	Visual perception, hand control and coordination between the two	ages 2-15	G	57
Developmental Test of Visual Perception	Eye-hand coordination, figure ground, constancy of shape, position in space and spatial relations	Nursery School to grade 3	G/I	57
Harris Tests of Lateral Dominance	Lateral dominance	ages 7-Adult	I	125
Huelsman Word Discrimination Test	Determines how well a child uses external configuration, length and internal design in perceiving words	2-8	G	103
Keystone Visual Survey Test, Telebinocular #46	Near and far point acuity, depth perception, muscle balance	All	I	86
Lincoln-Oseretsky Motor Development Scale	Static coordination, dynamic coordination of hands, general dynamic coordination, motor speed, simultaneous voluntary movements, performance without extraneous movements	ages 4-16	I	7
Merten's Visual Perception Test	Design copying, design reproduction, framed pictures, design completion, spatial recognition, visual memory	K-1	G	158
Riley Motor Problems Inventory	Small muscle coordination, laterality, gross motor coordination	Preschool to grade 5	I	158

VISUAL AND VISUAL MOTOR - 2

TEST	ABILITIES MEASURED	GRADE	TYPE	SOURCE
Movement Skills Survey	Body awareness, coordination, agility, strength, flexibility and balance	K-3	I	57
Perceptual Forms Tests	Perceptual maturity in eye-hand coordination	1-3	G	160
Primary Visual Motor Test	Visual-motor development	ages 4-8	I	66
Purdue Perceptual Motor Survey	Motor development and skills	ages 4-10	I	102
Slosson Drawing Coordination Test	Designed to identify a person with various forms of brain dysfunction or perceptual disorders where in eye-hand coordination is involved	ages 1-Adult	G	158
Southern California Sensory Integration Tests	Kinesthesia and tactile perception; figure ground visual perception, motor accuracy and space perception	ages 4-10	I	158
Spatial Orientation Memory Test	Retention and recall of directional orientation	ages 5-8	I	158